victorious Last-Day Christian. This would include his great faith in God, his passion for serving God and his unstoppable determination.

Whether you are a brand new believer or a seasoned saint, there will be nuggets of anointed truth waiting for you in the pages of this book, that will help guide you on the path to victory in the coming revival. Like the trying times that we currently live in, this revival will be filled with godless, antichrist opposition, but it will also filled with the greatest display of the grace, glory and miracles of God ever known to man.

So don't miss out on the preparation for your divine assignment. Read and study the truths contained in this book and gain the victory over opposition, and become equipped to flow in the miracle power of God in this very important hour.

Just as King David served God in his generation, so are you appointed and anointed for such a time as this.

Dr. Douglas J. Wingate
President and Founder of Life Christian University

ARE YOU A POWERFUL LAST-DAY CHRISTIAN?

IF YOU HAVE NO IDEA what that means, you must read this book, *Portrait of a Powerful Last-Day Christian*. God has called you to be His voice to a lost and dying world. I once heard it said, "If you don't stand for something, you will fall for anything!" We are living in very serious, unprecedented times, where truth is considered hate speech and the Bible is considered out-of-date. The attack from the enemy is coming from every side to try and disarm God's children. Society as a whole has bought into a lie that God's Word changes with culture, grace is now considered your ticket away from relationship with the Father, and worst of all, Christians have forgotten to occupy till He comes. Society is doing its very best to emphasize that Christians should be quiet lest we offend someone, and that "secular Christianity" is the new norm.

The Apostle Paul warned Timothy of these days in 2 Timothy 3:1-5: "Don't be naive. There are difficult times ahead. As the end approaches, people are going to be self-absorbed, money-hungry, self-promoting, stuck-up, profane, contemptuous of parents, crude, coarse, dog-eat-dog, unbending, slanderers, impulsively wild, savage, cynical, treacherous, ruthless, bloated windbags, addicted to lust, and allergic to God. They'll make a show of religion, but behind the scenes they're animals. Stay clear of these people" (The Message). This verse describes the moment that we now find ourselves in! We must rise up and take a stand for righteousness and purity. We must say, "Enough is enough! Devil, you can't have my family, my church, and my generation." Amazingly, we can see the similarities of today's battle in the story of a future King David when he loses everything at a place called Ziklag.

In his powerful new book, *Portrait of a Powerful Last-Day Christian*, my friend and mentor Pastor David Garcia has written a book that calls the Christian back to accountability and purpose. David Garcia is one of the greatest leaders I have ever met. He leads as an Apostolic voice with a passionate heart for the next generation. In his deep study of I Samuel 30, we are able to see how God can take the worst situation and restore your promises—even at a place called Ziklag! I believe that this book will stir the reader to not only believe that "with God all things are possible," but also to move to the next level of their journey with Christ. You can almost hear the dramatic music as Pastor David Garcia takes us through loss, fear, abandonment, self-forgiveness, and into restoration. This is a must-read for young Christians, the old believer, and everyone in between. This book will remove your excuse to not live victoriously. Once you conquer your Ziklag, then you are ready for promotion! This book is a step-by-step manual to rise up and take back what belongs to you. This book is destined to be a classic on the shelves of homes and churches! The restoration of Ziklag belongs to all of us. God has commanded us to rise up and chase down the enemy! This is your day to confront your enemy! Your family needs you to rescue them!

Patrick Schatzline, Evangelist
President of Mercy Seat Ministries
Author of *Why is God So Mad at Me?* and *I Am Remnant*

CONTENTS

"FATHER, IN JESUS'S NAME I pray for the one reading this book right now. I pray, Father, that you would bless them. I speak blessing over them right now, to be an overcomer with the wisdom not only to survive in this chaotic world, but the wisdom to know that their Egyptian is coming. That irrespective of what is happening right now, that God always sends an Egyptian to the obedient. God always send provision to the one who is hungry for God.

I PRAY FOR SPIRITUAL HUNGER right now, in the name of Jesus Christ of Nazareth. I pray for great wisdom in your life. I pray that you will be a pursuer of the things of God, and that your hunger will exceed your knowledge. I speak blessings upon your spirit, soul, and body—and financially.

IN JESUS' NAME, AMEN, AND Amen."

PREFACE

EVANGELICALS LIKE TO STRESS THE authority of the Believer. That is precisely what this book does. Many of you are intensely interested in end-time eschatology—the final events of history and the end of the world—and this book is written with you in mind also.

This is a very positive book for Christians to read. Literally, it is a handbook for overcoming in these final days! Our final days on this earth are something we should never be afraid of. The only ones who should be afraid are those who are not ready! But as born-again Believers, you are READY!

Sometimes fear and trepidation consume even Christians when the thought of the end-time days arises. What about my future? What about the economy? What about my family? What about my checkbook?

Relax. God is in control! God has purposes for you that you will not only be an overcomer, but you will be victorious, whether or not we have three hours left on this earth or 800 years!

As a Christian reader, you have already been bought with a price . . . His shed blood. So you have nothing to fear. President Franklin D. Roosevelt, during World War II, said: "We have nothing to fear, but fear itself!" That might not be in the Bible, but it is the essence of what God has already promised for you!

No matter what our news, television, and the internet proclaim for these end-time days, God has a real provision for you right now.

In this exciting book, you will learn how the devil is trying to scare you and take back what is rightfully yours. It is time to stand up and rightfully proclaim and take back what the devil has stolen from you. This mandate is of God. This is scriptural; and we will explore those positive, encouraging scriptures!

You are not in these final days to merely subsist and barely make it. You are one of God's chosen people! You are a literal son or daughter of God. You, as a joint heir, have certain God-given rights in these final days.

Many times, even Christians fall into the trap of the enemy and believe the "doom and gloom" of the end-time that Satan continues to harass us with. In this book, learn how to command the devil to leave you alone! God has much more in store for you. He has promotion and victory for YOU!

But thus says the LORD: "Even the captives of the mighty shall
be taken away, and the prey of the terrible be delivered;
for I will contend with him who contends with you,
and I will save your children".

Isaiah 49:25

God covets a communication relationship with you. I pray that my writing will assist you as you truly connect with God and the Holy Spirit as you receive a divine strategy to be victorious. Yes, a divine strategy can be yours as a last-day Christian.

As the final clock ticks down to the end of the world, you can be a shining light in a very dark world. You no longer have to hold down your head. You are victorious. You are a light-bearer in a dark world. People will literally seek you out for answers during these end-times.

As a last-day Christian, you will be someone who is looked up to, because you are not only a survivor, but a victorious overcomer. Yes, this may seem to be supernatural. And it is. The enemy must hand back to you everything he has stolen!

In this book, we will explore the Scriptures to find that God has intended for you to be victorious as a Last-Day Christian. Yes, God has promised this victory in the Scriptures. It is not just a feel-good, positive-thinking attitude; it is in the Word of God!

I have personally experienced this reality of victory. God still has many things for you to experience as a Last-Day Christian. No; it is not over. Your witness and your victory have only just begun. Your end-time victory has been foretold in the Holy Scriptures years ago. I will explore this fact in great detail.

The Word of God contains your victory! The Word of God says that you are a true overcomer! It is my personal prayer that you fully receive all the victories that God has for you as an overcomer!

There is no need for any fear to come against you in these end-time days! You are God's property. You are His ambassador on this earth during these final days. Live and act like an ambassador of the King. As you strengthen yourself in the Lord, learn to live above the circumstances and live like an heir to the King of Kings that you really are!

In this book, we will explore the journey that has taken place to attain your victory! The bottom line: God is on your side!

Ephesians 1:22-23 says: "And He put all things under His feet, and gave Him to be head over all things to the church, which is His body, the fullness of Him who fills all in all."

God's grace is for you. You are a man or woman after God's own heart! Psalm 37:23-24 reads, "The steps of a good man [or woman] are ordered by the Lord, And He delights in his [or her] way. Though he [or she] fall, he [or she] shall not be utterly cast down; For the Lord upholds him [or her] with His hand."

The fear of the Lord is the beginning of wisdom.

Proverbs 9:10

But fear of the circumstances in this world is not of God.

May this book be a victorious, Scriptural way to circumvent that fear that surrounds you every day, so you can be an overcomer!

A HANDBOOK FOR OVERCOMING

PORTRAIT OF A POWERFUL LAST-DAY CHRISTIAN is a very practical book on surviving emotionally, spiritually, and physically in these last days.

This is a handbook for overcoming. This book can be applied first and foremost to your family. We are living in a time of 2 Timothy 3:1–8, where people are unthankful, unholy, unloving, and unforgiving.

This book is a strategy by which you can keep your family saved. I speak Isaiah 49:25 to you, where the Lord says "I will contend with those who contend with your children, and I will save your children." This book is designed to help you and give you encouragement to take back what the devil has stolen from you. He has stolen some sons and daughters; he has stolen some husbands and wives.

We are living in economically uncertain times. We are living in times when there is upheaval with the dollar, upheaval with the euro, and the financial markets are bad. People have lost thousands of dollars in the stock market. This book is designed to help you connect with God, and He will give you a financial strategy on how to get out of debt and how to not be in financial ruin. Just as David recaptured, you are going to recapture all the monies that Satan has taken from you—better yet, to prevent you from losing that money in the first place.

Your family, your finances, and your future: Jesus is coming back soon! This book is a manual on how to live as a last-day Christian: how to maintain your focus. The world we live in is symbolized by Ziklag, which means "winding"; it means confusion. It's a lost world; it is under the influence of Satan. You are in this world, but you are not of this world. *Portrait of a Powerful Last-Day Christian* will help you not only to survive in this world but to be a person of excellence, to be a person who stands out, and to be a shining light of encouragement in a dark world. God bless you.

CHAPTER ONE

LAST-DAY CHRISTIANS OVERCOME

Now it happened, when David and his men came to Ziklag, on the third day, that the Amalekites had invaded the South and Ziklag, attacked Ziklag and burned it with fire, and had taken captive the women and those who were there, from small to great; they did not kill anyone, but carried them away and went their way. So David and his men came to the city, and there it was, burned with fire; and their wives, their sons, and their daughters had been taken captive. Then David and the people who were with him lifted up their voices and wept, until they had no more power to weep. And David's two wives, Ahinoam the Jezreelitess, and Abigail the widow of Nabal the Carmelite, had been taken captive. Now David was greatly distressed, for the people spoke of stoning him, because the soul of all the people was grieved, every man for his sons and his daughters. But David strengthened himself in the LORD his God.

1 Samuel 30:1–6

I WANT TO SHARE A prophetic word with you that God wants you to know: "The last-day Christian will take back from the enemy everything the enemy has stolen from him or her." That's what the last-day Christian is going to do. It begins with you . . . today.

You need to understand who you are in the Lord, so first we'll look at the kind of person that a last-day Christian will be.

THE PERSON

THE LAST-DAY CHRISTIAN WILL OVERCOME in the spirit of David. The last-day Christian will be an overcomer in the spirit of King David. How do I know this? Because the Bible says so. Let's look at some verses to see this.

He (Jesus) who has the key of David.

Revelation 3:7

Behold the lion of the tribe of Judah,
the root of David has prevailed.

Revelation 5:5

I Jesus, I am the root and the offspring of David.

Revelation 22:16

But thanks be to God who gives us the victory
through our Lord Jesus Christ.

1 Corinthians 15:57

Where does Jesus live? He lives in our hearts! So, if He lives in your heart, and Jesus is the root of David, then in Jesus we have the keys of David. We have the prevailing power of David. And we shall overcome like David overcame. Amen!

Let's look at this person, David. Let me share SIX things with you about David, from 1 Samuel 30:1-6:

1.   The last-day Christian will walk in the love of God. The final generation of Christ will walk in an overwhelming power of love, an Ephesians 3:16 love, where the length, the breadth, and the height of the love of God is displayed. I say this because the name David means "beloved." I want to declare to you today, and I don't care what has happened, I don't care how many mistakes you have made, I don't care how many times you might have backslidden: you are the beloved of the Lord. You are loved of God. You always will be loved of God. God cannot help but to love you, and God declares to you today that you need to get used to it. You need to tell yourself this every day: "I am loved! God loves me, and I am anointed to spread that love."

2.   The last-day Christian overcomes rejection. If you are the parent of a teenager, if you are a student in school, you probably already understand rejection. Look at 1 Samuel, Chapter 16. Write it down. I want you to get a picture of this. Saul is the king of Israel. God says, "I am now removing the kingdom from Saul. I am going to give it to a man after my own heart." The prophet Samuel said, "Where?" and God told him to go to the house of Jesse. Samuel's face lit up, because Jesse had

seven sons. They were all good looking. They were all specimens of virility and masculinity. Now it is the custom of the house that when you invite a guest, in Europe today, in America today, and especially in Israel back then, the whole household had to be there to greet the guest. Especially since Samuel tells Jesse, "one of your future sons is going to be the king." So when Samuel gets there, Jesse parades his sons. First comes Eliab. Eliab stands in front of him. This guy's been working out. He's got washboard abs. He is as handsome as can be in Hollywood (give me a little poetic license here), and Samuel says, "Lord, that's got to be him." The Lord says, "That is not him. For I am not like man. Man looks at the outside. I, the Lord, look on the inside." One by one, all of the sons are eliminated. Samuel is confused and says, "Lord there is something wrong." Then he asks Jesse if he has another son. Jesse says, "Yes, but I didn't ask him to come in because he is a little weird. He sings with a harp and he talks to sheep. He's kind of red-faced all the time. I didn't bother to bring him in."

Samuel says, "Bring him in." The minute David walks in, God says, "That's the man!"

So Samuel anoints David with oil. Imagine that the prophet of God comes to your house. Your dad is supposed to invite you in there, but he doesn't even bother to invite you in to greet the guest. That's rejection. David was seventeen at the time, and he suffered from his father's rejection, because his father didn't think he was good enough to welcome a prophet, much less be a candidate to be the king. The last-day Christian has no time to be beat down by rejection or the lack of approval. He or she is going to rise up, overcome rejection, and walk with a new confidence like never before. God says it is time to leave rejection behind and move ahead in the approval of the Lord.

3. This last-day Christian not only walks in love and overcomes rejection, but this last-day Christian is a giant killer. All of Israel is lined up for battle in 1 Samuel Chapter 17; every Sunday School child knows the story. There is a huge nine-foot giant confronting the army of Israel. Goliath is nine feet tall and has a javelin that weighs thirty pounds. All of Israel is cowering in their camp for forty days and forty nights. Goliath is defying the nation of Israel, basically saying, "You all are a bunch of chumps. You don't even dare to challenge me. I'm the champion of the Philistines. What do you have to offer?"

David hears Goliath and says (I'm paraphrasing here): "Who does this guy think he is? Let me at him. I'll whip him. I'll beat him in a couple of minutes. I won't fight with the arm and the flesh and the sword. I'll fight in the name of the Lord Jesus, in the name of God and the Lord of hosts of Israel."

David volunteers to fight, the soldiers bring him to King Saul, and all of a sudden, Saul says, "I'll let you take him on," and he loans David his own armor. David politely tries it out and says, "This won't work. I'm young. I've come to work for God with new ideas, new paradigms, and new strategies. I didn't come to do it the old way. I came to do it a new way. Nobody's ever had a single shot, but I'm going to kill him with a sling shot."

The Lord is saying to us today: "I'm raising up an army of teenagers and an army of young people who are going to slay the giants of America with new ideas, new paradigms, and new strategies." God is raising them up, and you might be one of them. Saul and the army saw the situation differently. They saw it with "impossibility" thinking, but David saw it with "possibility" thinking. They saw a giant who was too big to be conquered; David saw a giant who was so big, he couldn't miss him.

4. I think of 1 Samuel 18: the last-day person, man or woman of God, does everything in excellence and succeeds because of that. These last-day giant killers are not only anointed in love, they not only overcome rejection, but they will do everything in excellence.

Excellence means you do the best you can with all you have. Excellence means you go the extra mile. Excellence means that your middle name is, "Yes, it can be done. Yes, I will have it done." Excellence does not mean that you suffer with a disease called "excusitis": always excusing yourself. Excellence means when you hand in a report, you don't hand it in with chicken-scratch writing, crossed out all over the place: you hand it in with excellence. No cross-outs, type-outs, or spaced out. That's how you hand it in.

There are three levels of achievement. There is inferiority, mediocrity, and superiority. Excellence is superiority. It is work done in an impressive way: far above average, far above inferiority, far above mediocrity. Excellence is not only very accurate, it is stunningly excellent and beautiful. An example of this excellence can be found in

Daniel 6:3. Daniel was one of the three treasurers for the king when he was in captivity. It says that Daniel had an excellent spirit.

> Then this Daniel distinguished himself above the governors and satraps, because an excellent spirit was in him; and the king gave thought to setting him over the whole realm.
>
> Daniel 6:3

Excellence is work to perfection. It is not only work to perfection, it is distinguished work, that sets itself far above everything else. Another example would be 1 Kings 10:4-8. When the queen of Sheba goes to visit King Solomon, she describes how excellently Solomon's servants even set the tables.

> And when the queen of Sheba had seen all the wisdom of Solomon, the house that he had built, the food on his table, the seating of his servants, the service of his waiters and their apparel, his cupbearers, and his entryway by which he went up to the house of the Lord, there was no more spirit in her. Then she said to the king: "It was a true report which I heard in my own land about your words and your wisdom. However I did not believe the words until I came and saw with my own eyes; and indeed the half was not told me. Your wisdom and prosperity exceed the fame of which I heard. Happy are your men and happy are these your servants, who stand continually before you and hear your wisdom!
>
> 1 Kings 10:4-8

I would like to expand the definition of excellence to mean "work of the highest caliber; work that is not only superior, but highly impressive and with little room for improvement."

Excellence means you do your best. It means you talk right. It means you "talk in faith." To talk in faith means you talk the Word of God. You actually incorporate the Word of God in your conversation. Talking in faith also means you are very positive, very optimistic, and very confident. It means you speak expectantly, even though you don't see results now. You are speaking according to Romans 4:17, by calling things that are not as though they were.

You act right, and you act like you are going to succeed. The Bible says that David succeeded in everything he did because he "behaved himself wisely" (1 Samuel 18:5,14,15,30).

This terminology is an Old Testament phrase as translated by the King James Version of the Bible. It is found four times in reference to David in 1 Samuel chapter 18. The English Standard Version better captures the meaning in verse 5: "And David went out and was successful wherever Saul sent him." To behave yourself wisely is to conduct yourself in such a way that you will achieve your goals and you will be successful in your actions and your words.

5.   The last-day person overcomes persecution. He or she overcomes persecutions, and he overcomes anything that confronts him. In the seven chapters from 1 Samuel 19 through 1 Samuel 26, King Saul is hunting David. For seven chapters, Saul is after David, and David has every reason to defend himself and even to kill Saul. But David overcomes persecution; he is not overcome by

persecution. David is not only a giant killer; he is also a problem solver.

A giant is any big stronghold in your life. What do I mean by stronghold? In its basic meaning, it is anything that holds strongly to your thought life or your emotional life. For example: lust, greed, or anger. A giant is a behavioral problem that you cannot shake or overcome. It could be fear; there are giants of fear. When I say "giant killer," basically I am talking about 2 Corinthians 10:3–5:

> For though we walk in the flesh, we do not war according to the flesh. For the weapons of our warfare are not carnal but mighty in God for pulling down strongholds, casting down arguments and every high thing that exalts itself against the knowledge of God, bringing every thought into captivity to the obedience of Christ.

This means every thought: every mental thought and process that is anti-scriptural and that does not go along with the Word of God. You bring those thoughts under or into obedience, or in captivity to God's Word, through the power of the Holy Spirit and the grace of God (grace being God's enabling power in our lives).

David killing Goliath really shows us that—through the enabling power of God—we are David and the giant is whatever we are confronting. In reality, Jesus, through us, can kill that giant by His grace and by His power. We must be careful not to think that we have the power in ourselves to slay the giants. We really don't have any power in ourselves.

I'm reminded of John 15, when Jesus says, "without me you can do nothing." But at the same time, the Bible says to resist the devil (or resist the giant) and that you can do all things through Christ who strengthens you. So again, a giant killer is someone who brings into captivity anti-scriptural thought patterns and anti-scriptural behaviors and turns them into scriptural thoughts and behaviors, such as the fruit of the Spirit we find listed in Galatians 5:22–23.

David knew how to respect authority. He didn't touch the anointed or his authority. He knew how to respect someone in authority. The last-day Christian will be someone who reveres and honors authority and yet overcomes any problem, whether with authority or any other problem. Any mountain in the way, he will either go through it, around it, or break it down. He is going to overcome.

6. I see David in a field, writing the book of Psalms. This last-day person is powerful in the last days. The last-day Christian is not only anointed with love, overcomes rejection, is a giant killer, does things with excellence, overcomes problems and persecution; he is a worshiper. He is a praiser. He is not afraid to lift his hands up and shout for God. Praise is when you thank God for what He's done. Worship is when you thank God for who He is.

I've learned and taught this over the years: praise is when you thank God for what He's done; worship is when you thank God for who He is. In other words, praise is when you thank God for healing you; for providing money for you. But when you worship it is more intimate; you are directing it to Him. Now you are saying, "Jesus, you are my shepherd; you are Jehovah Jireh, my provider, Jehovah Rapha, my healer." It becomes more personal and more intimate and thus you are drawing closer to God.

When I'm in prayer in the house of God, my team has already won. I read the end of the Bible and Jesus is alive! Jesus whipped the devil and we put a chain around him. Why can't I worship God with excitement and joy? Don't tell me that you can get happy only when a sports team wins. Don't tell me that you can get happy only when your team wins the championship or first place. Sin is dead. The devil is bound. Jesus is alive and we live with Him, forever!

Don't think you are a man's man by sitting in church like a bump on a log, as if you cannot worship God. God is calling you to be a worshiper. Demons know the worshiper.

I had an unusual experience in the country of Hungary. My wife's interpreter was walking with me as I was prophesying to different people and casting out demons from different people. There was a gypsy woman. I will not forget her because her face was half red, and I saw demons on her. I told the interpreter to interpret and said, "You spirit of so and so get out!" And it screamed. My interpreter declared, "David!" (They call you by your first name there.) "David, the demon speaks English." I didn't get a chance to interpret. Every time I said something, the gypsy woman screamed. She was almost bringing up things.

Do you understand what I am saying?

Demons are trilingual. They've been to a university; they speak languages. You might say that they have Rosetta Stone software. They know who is anointed when they say, "Get out!" They leave. No interpretation is necessary. That is because, for God's glory, my wife and I are worshipers. Do you want to know what we do? We study and we worship God. The last-day Christian is going to be outstanding in God. You want to know something? That is YOU!

You might be saying, "That's not me. I'm not like that." In Christ Jesus, you are everything God meant you to be in Christ Jesus. But we need to recognize demons and know how to command demons to leave or flee!

Demons flee because of your intimacy with the Lord and your obedience. The Bible says in Mark 4:23–25: "The more you obey God, the more will be given to you. To him who has more will be given" (my paraphrase). Same thing in Luke 8:18. What does it mean "to him who has?" It means, to him who has obedience. What is given to the one who has obedience? He is given greater discernment; he is given greater anointing.

Here's the premise. If you are a doer of the Word (James 1:22), meaning you do your best to heed the logos (the written Word), then you qualify to hear the rhema (which is the specific spoken Word on our lives). Now you have moved into a deeper level of discernment and obedience. You have now moved into a Hebrews 5:12–14 level, which is a mature Christian who has his mature spiritual senses exercised to discern the difference between good and evil. Now you are no longer a young Christian who drinks milk only (only the logos). So when you flow in rhema and you have a great knowledge of the logos and a great knowledge of the rhema, then you can: (1) perceive and discern what demon is in operation, (2) you can speak directly to that demon who is oppressing that Christian and say directly to that demon, "In the name of Jesus, I command you to come out!" You can cast out that which is oppressing or inside that Christian. I did not say possessing, I said oppressing. The Greek word is daimonizomai

(Strongs #1139), meaning "to be exercised by a demon; to be vexed with a demon."[1]

You can help that Christian who has done everything they can to shake this giant, this stronghold in their life. They have repented, forsaken, and they still are plagued by strongholds such as lust or masturbation. I believe that deliverance from strongholds is a higher form of obedience and discipleship. Along comes someone who is a mature Christian and who ministers in deliverance. He commands that demon to leave that Christian in the name of Jesus and it is cast out.

THE PLACE

IT HAPPENED WHEN DAVID AND his men came to Ziklag. Let's take a brief look at 1 Samuel 27. Many times the battles of the present are seeds that we've sown in the past. Many times, what we are fighting now, we have to ask, "Jesus, am I reaping something I've sown?" Just like with David, the devil wants to remove your son, your daughter, your marriage, your finances, and everything else. You've got to ask yourself, "God, did I cause this?" Before you point your finger and say, "You dirty rat," point the three fingers back to yourself. Say to God, "Show me; did I do anything to cause this?" Let's take a flashback to 1 Samuel 27:1–12, where David is still on the run.

> And David said in his heart: "Now I shall perish someday by the hand of Saul.' There is nothing better for me than that I should speedily escape into the land of the Philistines; and Saul will despair of me, to seek me any more in any part of Israel: so shall I escape out of his hand." So David arose, and

[1] (*Biblesoft's New Exhaustive Strong's Numbers and Concordance with Expanded Greek-Hebrew Dictionary*. Copyright © 1994, 2003, 2006 Biblesoft, Inc. and International Bible Translators, Inc.)

went over with the 600 men that were with him to Achish, the son of Maoch, king of Gath.

David has killed Goliath, but now he joins Goliath's people. He defeats the Philistines, but now he joins the nation of the Philistines.

So David dwelt with Achish at Gath, he and his men, each man with his household, and David with his two wives, Ahinoam the Jezreelitess, and Abigail the Carmelitess, Nabal's widow. It was told to Saul that David had fled to Gath; so he sought him no more. Then David said to Achish, "If I have now found favor in your eyes, let them give me a place in some town in the country that I may dwell there. For why should your servant dwell in the royal city with you?" Achish gave him Ziklag that day.

The immediate reference was that King Achish gave David the city of Ziklag. Ziklag was the devil's gift. Never settle for the devil's gifts. Never take the devil's gifts. Never settle for assignments given to you by the enemy. An assignment from God is something that God gives you to fulfill. It can be a person or it can be a task. For example, your assignment might be to teach a Sunday School class. Your wife is your assignment. The devil can also give you a task or an assignment. He can give you an unsaved wife, and we know according to 2 Corinthians 6:14 that you would then be unequally yoked. Unequally yoking yourself with an unbeliever would be to take the devil's gifts. Taking on the devil's assignment would be choosing a ministry or doing a ministry, that, while it might be good and godly, is not the one that God has given you to do at this moment.

For example, maybe your time is limited. We make an announcement in church on Sunday that we need workers for the evangelistic outreach the following Saturday. You feel burdened or manipulated to join that ministry, although God never asked you to join that ministry. Now you have no time on Saturday with your son or your daughter and you now neglect them. Satan is always offering us gifts to distract us from the real assignments of God, hoping we will take them. If we do, then we will not be spending our energy and time with the people we need to be with.

Continuing with the scripture: "Therefore Ziklag has belonged to the kings of Judah to this day. Now the time that David dwelt in the country of the Philistines was one full year and four months." That is sixteen months that David stayed in Ziklag. Now watch what happens.

When David was given Ziklag, what he would do is go from there out and raid the nations. See 1 Samuel 27:6–12. David and his men would use Ziklag as a base for going out to attack the enemies of Israel, for example the Geshurites, the Girzites, and the Amalekites. These are the same people who would later on burn Ziklag. The key is this: you reap what you sow. David would kill many people. It is said in verse 11 of 1 Samuel 27 that when David would raid he would not leave anybody alive.

By that act alone, when the Amalekites came months later to put an end to these raids, David deserved to reap the death of his wives and children. But instead, by the grace of God (God's enabling power), God kept David's children and wives alive even though David had sowed murder and should have reaped murder. What goes around comes around. What came around for David, although he deserved for his family to be murdered, was they were protected; the Amalekites didn't kill them. That was the grace and mercy of God for David to continue to have his family.

If David had gotten what he deserved, they would have been murdered. It's the grace of God that is with the last-day Christian. David would save neither man nor woman alive, to bring news to Garth, saying, "Lest they should inform on us, saying, 'Thus David did.' Thus was his behavior all the time he dwelt in the country of the Philistines. So Achish believed David."

Let's get to this place called Ziklag.

The last-day Christian understands the prophetic message of Ziklag. Ziklag is the place of human mistakes. I want to emphasize that again: The last-day Christian understands that the meaning of Ziklag is the place of human mistakes. Have you ever made a mistake? Of course you have. I have blown it. People have blown it, sown it, and will soon reap it. The quicker we find out about our sin, the faster God will change the harvest. This is the place of human mistakes. This is where the last-day Christian understands that he or she is human. If it weren't for the grace of God, we wouldn't have anything. This means that if God has given you grace, then you give somebody else grace. You walk in forgiveness. Be patient with yourself. Be patient with others. Young people need to be patient with the elderly. The elderly need to be patient with the young people.

We all should display a sign saying, "I have not arrived. I am still under construction. I am still being built up! God has not finished with me yet." First Peter 2:5 says: "You also, as living stones, are being built up a spiritual house, a holy priesthood, to offer up spiritual sacrifices acceptable to God through Jesus Christ."

The next time your spouse makes a mistake, and before you point your finger at him or her, point it at yourself. Your wrong is not far behind. If you don't believe me, your teenage son or daughter will say the same thing to you: "Dad, but you're always . . ."

I have made some big mistakes in four decades of ministry. For example, there was a long season where I was so involved in the church that I failed to see the emotional needs of my wife. She was my partner, not only at home, but at church as well. But I failed to see all the attacks of the devil, the problems we were dealing with. I wanted my wife to play a role in the church ministry, but her involvement was detrimental to her emotional well-being. She would say "I don't want to go," but I would want her to share my problems. I forgot that my wife had personal needs. I was consumed by the church. I was putting the emotional needs of the people above the emotional needs of my wife.

I think one of my biggest human weaknesses as a leader and a pastor of a church is that in my endeavor to help people, I can be too merciful. Instead of disciplining people strongly enough when they need it—cutting out a cancer, removing somebody from a position—I tend to wait too long. By the time I remove them, the harm has already been done: they have caused division and have caused people to leave the church.

Also, I realized a few years ago that I was an "approval junkie." I actually welcomed and looked forward to the compliments of people. I had gotten to the place that if people didn't compliment me, I would feel hurt and feel rejected. One day I came to God, and He told me that I was just trying to coddle a root of rejection in my life. My parents, although very loving with each other, weren't too affectionate with me and my two brothers. We all craved the approval of our father and mother, who were both always working. They left at seven in the morning and didn't return until five at night. So I learned to lean on the praises of other people. Soon I became so addicted to praises that I got to the place where I expected the praises of people. This is not good; it is sin. All our approval must come from God. All our praise must come from God. It must come from my sonship with Him—all approval comes from Him, not from my pastoring.

What do we learn from Ziklag?

Looking at chapter 27, we see three powerful truths.

1.   David is fatigued and fearful. David is tired. He is exhausted; he is stressed out. I want to prophesy to you that the last-day Christian will fight a lot of stress and fear. We are living in times of exhaustion. Life in our modern Western societies is stressful, and most pastors are very stressed. Maybe you are tired and weary even now? We are fighting more demons than ever before, so we must learn how to rest in the Lord.

To rest in the Lord, as outlined in Hebrews chapter 4, is to have freedom from all anxiety, fear, and worry. We rest in the Lord first and foremost through our personal devotion to God; we have to be intimate with the Lord. In 1 John 4:18, the Word of God tells us that "perfect love casts out fear." You won't know that perfect love unless you are a worshipper and a praiser, unless you draw close to God. You have to be in the Word of God and you have to spend a great deal of time worshiping God for who He is. Then you will get to the place where there is no more anxiety in you. You will truly know Romans

8:28: "And we know that all things work together for good to those who love God, to those who are called according to His purpose."

If I love God and I'm intimate with Him, I will discern His purposes for me. If I love God and stay in His purposes, then I will not be subject to the fears and the anxieties that are prevalent today.

2. When you are tired and stressed, you will have a tendency to give in to human reasoning. In verses 2–5, David is so tired and he is so messed up. He is tired of running and he thinks he has it all figured out. "Saul won't attack me if I join the Philistines," he thinks.

Teenagers often think that if they join the inner circle in their high school, if they act just like the cool kids do, then maybe they won't get picked on anymore. They think to themselves: "If I become just like everybody else and party just like everybody else, and if I get high like everybody else, maybe they will leave me alone and they will accept me."

I say to these teenagers: You don't need acceptance from those other students; you need acceptance from God! If you join them, you will have to play the fool. I understand these feelings, though, because there was a period of time before I accepted Christ when I also wanted acceptance. When I was unsaved, in the late fifties, we would visit my maternal grandparents in Cuba. On one trip, a man molested me, and then he made me watch his parents doing sexual things. So at the young age of only eight and a half, I began to have extremely lustful patterns of thought, and I always felt ashamed of this. I tried to tell my parents, but this was a time when children were to be seen and not heard. I had nightmares. I always felt shame. Mentally and emotionally, this could have destroyed me.

Moving the clock forward: God saved me in a hotel room. I had a Damascus-road experience in June of 1974 at the Fletcher Avenue Days Inn in Tampa, Florida.

I had already read Hal Lindsey's book, *The Late Great Planet Earth*. I was reading a Gideon Bible, and a Pentecostal book by Hobart Freeman, *The Angels of Light*. This reading helped me to overcome some demonic oppression that I had acquired from my dad, who, being a Freemason, had "innocently" taken me to a spiritist temple, where I was introduced to some demons. After that, I couldn't sleep without having a nightmare and waking up screaming. Every dream ended up with me falling off a cliff and breaking into a thousand pieces.

These experiences all came together in June. I had graduated from consulting a Ouija board to consulting a cup. I would ask this cup, "Should I make this decision?" If the answer was a yes, it would move in one direction. If it was a no, it would move in the opposite direction.

To my great annoyance, the motel housekeeping maids wouldn't clean my room. This was because I always had the television blasting, I had the "Do Not Disturb" sign up, and the curtains drawn. This upset me, and I had complained to the front desk. One night I heard a voice. I thought it was the voice of my spirit guide (which was a demon, of course). The voice said, "David, if you would turn your television off, turn the sign around to request the maid to clean your room, and open your curtains, then the maids will come in and change your sheets and give you new towels." So I did as the voice suggested, and when I came back from business the next day, sure enough, I had clean sheets and new towels.

What I didn't know is that the Holy Spirit was setting me up. That night I was reading *The Angels of Light.* It was talking about ESP, yoga, talking to the dead—and asking if these things were from God or Satan? I was so consumed with rage that this "Pentecostal" would write such things, that I was going to track him down and tell him off. I never finished the book, though, because somewhere it mentioned Deuteronomy 18:9–35, and I managed to find that passage in the Gideon Bible. It said, "Do not make your sons and daughters walk through fire, do not talk to the dead, all that do these things are an abomination to God." It said I was going to hell.

In the book *The Late Great Planet Earth,* I went back and reread the chapter where Hal Lindsey talked about being born again. And I told God that I wanted to be born again.

Now, I grew up a Catholic, with certain traditional prayers that simply did not work. The Holy Spirit told me—the same one who had told me to put up the maid sign, to turn off the television, and to open the curtains—that same voice told me: "David, if you will open up the curtains to your heart and ask Me, I will give you new sheets and clean towels for your life." So that is exactly how I prayed. I had read in John chapter 3 in the Gideon Bible about being born again. I thought, "I am like this guy, Nicodemus," and I wanted to be born again. I got on my knees and I said, "Jesus, I'm so sorry I talk to the dead, to spirits. Forgive me. I want to be born again. Forgive me of adultery (at that time I had numerous encounters of which I am not proud). I truly repented and I said, "God, give me new sheets and towels in my heart."

The Lord used that simple physical illustration to save me; He came into my life and I have never ever been the same again.

A few months later, around October of 1974, I was reading a classic book called, *What Would Jesus Do?* I asked Him, "Lord, what would you have me to do to be more like You?" The Lord told me, "You must forgive _____". _____ was the man who had molested me in Cuba. I said, "God, You forgive him." Suddenly, I saw a cross in my spirit. Jesus pointed out the line that went straight up, and said, "I died for what you did wrong to Me. I died for your sin. You are free from the penalty of hell." I said, "I got it." He said, "You see the line going across?" I said, "Yes." He said, "I died for what _____ did to you. I died for what people did to you. You are free from the penalty of bitterness." I declared, "Jesus, I let _____ go, I forgive him." That was the beginning of my knowing how much Jesus loves me and accepts me.

I have since learned that everyone needs admiration and affirmation. Affirmation is when God thanks you for who you are; admiration is when God thanks you for what you've done.

One day I was reading Matthew 3, where it says, "this is my beloved Son, in whom I am well pleased." I saw that God affirmed Jesus and He had not even started His ministry yet. The Father accepted Jesus simply for who He was. Jesus had lived thirty years without sinning, but He had not yet started His ministry. That was the day when I realized that God loves me and accepts me for who I am; He admires me and loves me when I accomplish my mission and even when I don't accomplish my mission. It has nothing to do with my performance. It has everything to do with His eternal love.

I'm not talking about looking for society's affirmation. There was a time when David had to act like a crazy man. He had to spit on his beard, crawl around on all fours, and make weird noises. Everyone said about him, "That guy is crazy!" Now, I don't mind if people think that I'm crazy in my human reasoning, if actually I'm being crazy for Jesus. My point is this: you can't adapt to the world's systems and then expect God's blessings. If you're in business, you need to understand this: you cannot adapt to the world's methods and then expect Godly rewards.

3.   In verses 6 through 12, David is in the place of compromise and confusion. The last-day Christian cannot afford to live in compromise and confusion. That's what Ziklag means. *Ziklag* means "compromise and confusion." You don't want your family in Ziklag. You don't want a future son-in-law who is "Mr. Ziklag." You don't want your daughter marrying Mr. Ziklag. You don't want your son marrying Ms. Ziklag either. You don't want someone who is in confusion and compromise.

Ziklag literally means "winding downward." It's like one of those new rides at the amusement park. It's going up and then going down. Everybody likes the up part, but then you know you're going to go, "Ahhh," and your heart is going to feel like it's coming out of your chest. So if you don't want the "Ahhh," don't get on the ride. The last-day Christian doesn't get on those kind of rides. You ask me, "What do you mean by that, pastor?" I mean, do not give into compromise and confusion. Don't be like everybody else on the roller coaster of our culture, and you won't reap what everybody else gets.

This is what God is saying, "The mistakes of the past must be realized and corrected to guarantee a better future." The mistakes of your past must be realized and corrected to guarantee a better future for yourself. God never checks your past to determine your future.

We know that; we've heard that before. The only time God has you look into your past is when there is unresolved conflict somewhere. Please listen carefully. The only time God has you look into your past is if you have:

1. Unresolved conflict; or

2. A bad harvest. But if you can fix it and re-seed it, then you can change the harvest. David never did this. So he walks into a burnt city with no wives, no sheep, and no money. He looked like a lot of Christians today—broke, busted, and disgusted.

When something bad happens, ask, "God, did I cause this? Am I reaping something that I've sown? If I did, I want to make it right."

The quicker you make it right, the quicker the harvest will change!

I used to think you can't do anything about a harvest. Yes, you can! If you are not saved today, if you're not a Christian today, or if you just believe in God, but you are doing your "church thing," the quicker you get right with God, the quicker your harvest will change!

THE PERIOD

THE BIBLE SAYS, "NOW IT happened when David and his men came to Ziklag on the third day." Not the fourth day, not the second day; it was the third day. You need to understand something. What do we mean by the third day? The last-day Christian prophetically under-stands that we are living in the third day of God's sovereign calendar.

This comes from Hosea chapter 6:1–2: "Come, and let us return to the Lord; For He has torn, but He will heal us; He has stricken, but He will bind us up. After two days He will revive us; on the third day He will raise us up." And read 2 Peter 3:8: "But beloved, do not forget this one thing. With the Lord, one day is like a thousand years." So remember, on the second day, after two days, after two thousand years, God will revive us.

Revival is coming worldwide.

We are living in the end.

But on the third day, resurrection is coming. We are going to be raptured out of this place. The first two thousand years have already gone by. The next thousand years will be the Thousand-year Reign of the Lord. We are overdue for a trip to heaven. We are living near that last trip, my friend. We are living in that last third day. It is time!

In the Bible, the number 3 represents the following things:

1. **Restoration.** Prophetically, the last-day Christian must understand that every denomination is a truth that was lost but has been restored. For example, in 1517, Martin Luther rediscovered the truth that "the just shall live by faith." But instead of running with God on that truth, they made a denomination out of it; these Christians are called the Lutherans. Then in the 1600s, the Baptists rediscovered that we need water baptism. But instead of continuing to move forward, they made the Baptist denomination. In the 1700s, the Presbyterians discovered the presbytery and the laying on of hands, and they made the Presbyterians.

I want you to know that we are in the very last of the restoration. While the chapter divisions in our modern Bibles are not inspired, Acts 3:19–21 says that Jesus cannot come back until the restoration of all things. What is God restoring? The last-day Christian realizes that God is restoring the prophet and the apostle back into the Body of

Christ where they belong. He understands that in Ephesians 2:20, the church is built on the foundation laid by the prophet and the apostle.

> Now, therefore, you are no longer strangers and foreigners, but fellow citizens with the saints and members of the household of God, having been built on the foundation of the apostles and prophets, Jesus Christ Himself being the chief cornerstone.
>
> Ephesians 2:19-20

The last-day Christian understands that we've always had pastors. What does a pastor do? He guards his people. They walk in the love of God.

Then the church moved on, and from the 1700s up until the 1960s we had the age of the evangelist. What do evangelists do? They are the hand of God. They gather. They get the people saved. They are the hand of God doing signs and wonders.

But God kept moving on, and from the 1960s to the 1980s you had the teachers. Teachers ground people. You have Joyce Meyers, Kenneth Copeland, and great teaching ministries spread out all over the place. They give the doctrine of God and they ground people in the truth.

At the beginning of the 1990s you have the restoration of the prophets. Prophets give the guidance of God. They are pointers. The prophets offer the mind of God.

In this day and age, we are at the age of the apostle. The apostle governs. An apostle is a father. He establishes the church and he shows the heart of God.

This is what God is doing right now. God is raising up spiritual fathers to mentor a last-day army of protégés. Last-day Christians need to make sure they are in a church that has the prophetic and apostolic flowing in their lives to release their gifts and then they can move on.

2.   **Resurrection.** God is saying to you today, "Whatever your dead dreams were, whatever your dead desires were, it's time to resurrect them. I'm going to rapture you in full fulfillment of what I've called you to do." You will be everything that God calls you to be.

God is saying to you today, "Whatever your dead dreams were, whatever your dead desires were, it's time to resurrect them." It's time to reread the things you wrote down, and to ask God to show you the desires you had a few years ago. It is time to pursue what you were called to do before Jesus comes. You want to go into eternity hearing, "Well done, thou good and faithful servant, enter into the joy of the Lord" (Matthew 25:21). It's time to be a finisher of what God was trying to start years ago.

Ask God to reveal to you the many dreams and desires, the many assignments that for one reason or another you failed to finish, or failed to start.

3.   **Revival.** The last-day Christian moves in revival. He or she functions in the gifts of the Spirit. They function in their office gifts. They function in their Holy Spirit gifts. They function in their giftedness, and they are being used; because if you don't use it, you lose it. They

are rightly aligned to God's will and rightly assigned in God's place.

4. **Approval.** The last-day Christian knows that this is the day of the end of rejection and the beginning of acceptance. This is the end of feeling sorry for yourself. This is the end of, "What are they going to think of me?" Forget what are they going to think of you. What's God going to think of you? The last-day Christian understands that the number three means, "Well done, thy good and faithful servant. Enter into the joy of your salvation."

5. **Completion.** Read John chapter 2, where Jesus attended a wedding at Cana. On the third day during that wedding his mother Mary says, "Son, help them." Jesus replied, "What have I to do with you?" In John 2:5 (listen up, Catholics and former Catholics), Mary tells them, "whatever Jesus says to you, you have to do." All of a sudden they needed wine and Jesus turns water into wine. Normally, you serve the best wine first and then the worst wine last. After Jesus turned the water into wine, the man said, "Usually you serve the best first and the latter last. But, you have saved the best wine for last."

We are in the third day, so this story teaches us that the greatest revelations are going to come now. I believe with all my heart that the reasons we are having an increase in Bible prophecies is because in His sovereignty, knowing that Jesus is coming soon, God is allowing the Holy Spirit to reveal to us the deep profound mysteries in the book of Revelation and the things of the last days.

I believe that God is putting all the pieces of the puzzle together. I don't think God is going to allow any one denomination or any one person to have the whole truth. I think that He purposely reveals in bits and pieces so that we need each other. We are getting more understanding about the last days, Bible prophecy, about the deep truths of the Kingdom of God, and God's purposes, because the hour is late—Jesus is coming soon!

The greatest revelations are going to come now. The greatest move of God is going to come now. The greatest harvest is going to come now. The best is yet to come! Your greatest hour is coming now!

CHAPTER TWO

STRENGTHEN YOURSELF IN THE LORD

WE CONTINUE OUR STUDY IN 1 Samuel 30:1–8.

> Now it happened, when David and his men came to Ziklag, on the third day, that the Amalekites had invaded the South and Ziklag and burned it with fire, and had taken captive the women and those who were there, from small to great; they did not kill anyone, but carried them away and went their way. So David and his men came to the city, and there it was, burned with fire; and their wives, their sons, and their daughters had been taken captive.
>
> Then David and the people who were with him lifted up their voices and wept, until they had no more power to weep. David's two wives, Ahinoam the Jezreelites, and Abigail the widow of Nabal the Carmelite, had been taken captive. Now David was greatly distressed, for the people spoke of stoning him, because the soul of all the people

was grieved, every man for his sons and his daughters. But David strengthened himself in the Lord his God.

In this passage, God is giving us a model that we need to run after, a portrait of a powerful, last-day Christian.

This is a time of crisis in David's life. The enemy has stolen everything, and now it's up to David to take it back. God is saying, "I am calling you to take back what the devil has stolen from you." This is what God is saying to you today!

"Strengthening yourself in the Lord," as David did, means that you begin to confess God's Word. You begin to confess out loud God's promises. That even though something has been stolen from you; even though there is an apparent failure in your life, you begin to confess who God is through worship. You worship Him; you reiterate your vision. You reiterate your purposes in God, and you praise and worship Him, and in this way you receive His strength to go on. We see this in verses 7 and 8:

> Then David said to Abiathar the priest, Ahimelech's son, "Please bring the ephod here to me." And Abiathar brought the ephod to David. So David inquired of the Lord, saying, "Shall I pursue this troop? Shall I overtake them?" He answered him, "Pursue, for you shall surely overtake them and without fail recover all."

That's a word for you today . . . right now!

Pursue, because you shall surely overtake them and—without fail—recover all.

In verse one, we've already studied about the person. We learned that the last-day overcomer knows that he is beloved of the Lord, and so he overcomes rejection and self-pity. Then we learned about the place, Ziklag. The last-day overcomer overcomes confusion; he overcomes the downturns in his life. Then we learned about the time period. The powerful last-day Christian knows that we are living in the third day. The third day is the day of resurrection. The third day is the day of restoration. The third day is the day of revival.

Now let's look at the PEOPLE.

The Amalekites are symbolic of the devil. They represent the devil. Why do I say this? The powerful last-day Christian knows his enemies, their tactics, and knows how to defeat them. As 2 Corinthians 2:11 says, "We are not ignorant of the devil's devices." We are not ignorant of the devil's methods. I'm going to give you those methods that he is using right now. Let me show you four things about the Amalekites, which are also four things about the devil.

1. The Amalekites always oppose Israel and the plan of God. When the Israelites came out of Egypt, no sooner had they crossed the Red Sea, in Exodus 17, than the Amalekites attacked them. The Israelites had no choice in the matter. They had hardly any weapons, and the Amalekites attacked them. In Exodus 17:8, we read: "Amalek came and fought with Israel in Rephidim." The enemy is always at war with you. You need to understand that you are in a war. You didn't volunteer for this war; the devil volunteered you for this war.

This is a war between your spirit and your flesh. This is a war between God's people and the devil's people. This is a war between the angels of God and the angels of Satan. This is a war between us and demons, and we win. We are not "winning"—we have already won. You need to understand that. Satan opposes the people of God. You need to understand that the devil hates your guts. You need to understand that right now! He would like to send you to hell. He would like nothing better than for you to bake in the lake with him for all of eternity.

You must not give into that!

We need to understand that there has always been a war between God and Satan. God won the war on the cross of Calvary. But now, as Christians, we need to walk out that victory.

First of all, there is a war between our flesh and our *spirit.*

> Walk in the Spirit, and you shall not fulfill the lust of the flesh. For the flesh lusts against the Spirit, and the Spirit against the flesh; and these are contrary to one another, so that you do not do the things that you wish. But if you are led by the Spirit, you are not under the law.
>
> Galatians 5:16–18

If you allow yourself to be dominated by your fallen nature, then you will not fulfill God's will. Paul elaborates on the works of the flesh in Galatians 5 verses 19–21. I won't go through the whole list, but if you allow adultery, fornication, lust, drunkenness, jealousies, or contentions to dominate your life, if you continue in these things, then you will not inherit the Kingdom of God. The war is between your flesh and your spirit. The Holy Spirit wants you to walk in, or be dominated by, the fruit of the spirit, which is Galatians 5:22–23: love, joy, peace, patience, gentleness, and so on.

There is a war between Satan's people and God's people. Satan has people he controls; they are always trying to infiltrate our churches.

We need the gift of discerning of spirits like never before so that we can tell them apart.

There is a war between the angels of God and the angels of Satan. If our spiritual eyes were opened up in any of our worship services, we would see God's angels fighting the devil's angels. The angels of God are always trying to bring us the message of God and Satan's angels are always trying to stop those angels (see Daniel 9–10).

There is a war between us and demons. Demons are agents of Satan on earth; they are here to execute the will of Satan on people. We are to cover people using the weapons of God. Our weapons are the Word of God, the Name of Jesus, the Blood of Jesus, and the Sword of the Spirit (which is the *rhema* Word of God). Through Jesus's Name we have victory.

2. The Amalekites were called by God to be destroyed. They were called by God to be exterminated down to the last man, woman, and child. In Exodus 17:13, Joshua defeats Amalek. Then in the next verse, Exodus 17:14, look at what God says: "Then the Lord said to Moses, 'Write this for a memorial in the book and recount it in the hearing of Joshua, that I the Lord will utterly blot out the remembrance of Amalek from under heaven.'"

Did you know that when God promises something, He is going to do it! Please learn a great lesson from God. Jesus defeated Satan in I John 3:8: "For this purpose was the son of God manifest that he might destroy the works of the evil one." Why does it say "might"? Because everything Jesus does, He does through us. We have to finish what He started. Hebrews 2:14 tells us that Jesus might destroy the works of the enemy. Again, why am I saying this? The Amalekites were called to be destroyed.

3. The Amalekites survived because of the compromise of God's people. God's people didn't do what they were supposed to do. God's plans can be limited by human obedience.

Mark 6:1–4 says that Jesus could do no mighty works in Capernaum because they said he was just a carpenter's son. Due to their disobedience and dishonor, the people of Capernaum limited God from doing mighty works such as raising the dead and opening blind eyes. But little ole' you and me can finish the work of God by doing the opposite. We can walk in obedience and we can honor God. What is the greatest commandment that Jesus gave us? Go into all the world and preach the gospel, making disciples.

But we must realize that it is not just "little ole' me." In Christ Jesus, we are very strong. We might be humanly insignificant (see 1 Corinthians 1:26: not many are mighty, not many are noble"), but we have a great commission directly from Jesus, and when we participate in missions, when we participate in soul-winning and making disciples, then we are finishing what God started.

People always ask, "How come bad things happen, and why does God allow them to happen?" Well, often it's because He was waiting on you to do something.

In 1 Samuel 15:17–33, God tells Saul, the King of Israel, to destroy all of the Amalekites, including the sheep, cattle, and children: everything they had. (Before you think he is a cruel God, it's better for those children to die early and go to heaven than to live on and wind up in hell. Don't you stand in judgment of God.) But Saul allows Agag, the king of the Amalekites, to live. What you don't know is that Saul more than likely allowed a remnant of the Amalekites to live, along with Agag. How do we know this?

In 1 Samuel 27, verse 8 and onward, we read that David would go from Ziklag and raid the Gershurites, the Girzites, and the Amalekites. Wait a minute; I thought Saul got rid of all of them. I thought he only left Agag the king, and then Samuel killed him. No, there had to have been a remnant of people.

Whenever you discover a giant in your life, a problem in your life, don't defeat it 90 percent or 92 percent. You better get rid of the whole thing, or else it will come back and haunt you. God is not saying to almost get rid of it, or just about finish it off. There is no "just about it! You get rid of the whole thing. There is no compromise in God, or it will come back to haunt you.

I can give a couple of real-life examples of someone who tried to compromise with God and it came back to haunt them.

I will speak in very general terms. The first one was a Christian family. The father battled with an immorality. I won't go into what it was, but it is sufficient that it was immoral. He was very carnal, in that he knew that it was wrong. He often confessed it was wrong, but he kept frequenting and kept going back to the places that would feed this lustful desire that he had. As a result, today he has lost his family and lost his marriage. It is so sad because he was so talented and so gifted by God.

The other example involved a woman who was married. She began to compromise because in her opinion her emotional needs were not being met by her husband, and so she began to receive the compliments of men around her. She would be convicted in church, would cry and come to the altar and repent. Eventually, she had an affair, then multiple affairs. Regardless of what church she went to, it was always the same. She would compromise with being too touchy with men, being too comfortable with men when her husband wasn't around. It led to tremendous turmoil within her family. Though extremely talented, she has never fully achieved what God wanted her to achieve. We can only pray that one day this woman will turn around.

Ephesians 1:22–23 reads: "And He put all things under His feet, and gave Him to be head over all things to the church, which is His body, the fullness of Him who fills all in all."

As we have seen with these two examples, Jesus is limited by the Church. God the Father put all things under the feet of Jesus, and gave Jesus to be the head over all things to the Church, which is His body, the fullness of Him who fills all in all.

All things are under the feet of Jesus. So all things should be under our feet, including the devil. But instead of being under our feet, too often he is on top of our head. Just as Saul let the Amalekites slide, we let sin slide. Every now and again, we cuss a little bit, drink a little bit, and check out the women a little bit. It's the little bit that will send you to hell! You need to be careful. The powerful last-day Christian has no compromise with sin.

4.   The Amalekites were characterized by cruelty and cowardice. Satan is a coward. You read that right. He is a coward! He loves to abort little babies. Did you know that little babies try to run away from the suction cup? Did you know that they try and get away, and that they scream? Do you know that if one hundred percent of

those mothers heard what was going on inside, they would repent and ball in tears? Yet, we've murdered so many millions of babies. People are always saying, "I'm against the war overseas," yet they are for the war against babies. We will spend millions of dollars for a beached whale, yet we will slaughter millions of babies. God is bringing judgment on America if we keep it up. What defense does that little one have? It's not a fetus, by the way; it's a human being! The Supreme Court cannot make up their mind. When it's a baby in the womb, they call it a fetus. Yet, if you murder that woman, they will charge you with a double homicide. Somebody wearing the black robes needs to get their act together. They need to wake up and deal with reality.

In 1 Peter 5:8, the devil walks around like a roaring lion seeking whom he may devour. Some people say that the old lions that roar don't have any teeth. You haven't lived in Africa; I have. Those lions can tear you apart. We lived there; we know. You need to understand and write this down. Second Corinthians 2:11 says, "We are not ignorant of the devil's devices." Allow me to share some of his devices that he is doing in your life right now. Let me prophesy devices he has always used, as well as his new ones.

The devil loves to cast *doubt* about your salvation. He loves to say you are not. He loves to say don't believe this and that, that you will never get healed, or you will never do that. If he can't get you with doubt, he will get you with distraction. He will get you to look at something else.

Another is *distraction*. Recently I went out to eat at one of my favorite restaurants. You would never know we were in a recession, because that place was packed. People were sitting and gazing at the televisions. I stood up, and a woman looked at me and her eyes told me, "Get out of the way, my horse is running." I said, "I'm sorry." I mean, I was in front of her god . . . I mean her horse. I had to move. *Distraction* will get you out of your assignment.

Then there is *deception*. If he (the devil) cannot distract you, he will deceive you. He will lie to you. He will get you into false doctrine. That's why if you have some strange or unfamiliar Bible books, before you jump into the pool, would you please ask me what kind of pool it is. Don't start a Bible study with some fly-off-the-handle doctrine and you didn't check with your pastor. We know what we are doing; we are mechanics of the soul. Don't ask me to fix your car. But I will fix your soul.

Then there is *discouragement*. The devil is having a heyday with this one. He is making people feel like nothing. He has made unemployed men feel like garbage. He is making young people feel like they don't have a father, and God doesn't love them. He's making the singles feel that this is the loneliest time of the year. The devil is the one telling you, "You have nothing going on and there are no good-looking men in the church. Nobody is every going to marry you in that church. You better go to the bar, girl, where you were before."

Then there is *division*. He is causing division in churches. He is causing division in homes. Strife and arguments over the stupidest things. Have you found yourself arguing over the dumbest things lately? You ask yourself, "What are we arguing about?" "I don't know, but I was right." "Right about what?" "I don't know, but I was right!"

Then there is *destruction.* John 10:10 says Satan is out to rob, to kill, and to destroy. He would love to destroy your character. He wants to destroy your marriage. He is after your sons and he is after your daughters. He would like to deflower every virgin in the house. I want you to know that right now.

Then there is *disease.* The purpose of disease is to remove Christians from their assignments. If the devil can't stop you from going to heaven, he will sure enough try to stop you from getting someone else to heaven.

But I have a God who bought the victory for us. He rose from the dead. We are guaranteed not only eternal life, but for you to be able to bring thousands with you.

THE PLUNDER

What do I mean by plunder? I mean highway robbery. The passage says, "taken captive." That's what the devil is out to do. He took wives, he took children, he took the money, he took the finances, he took everything. If you let the devil, he will take your clothes. He will take your house and your checkbook. You need to understand that the devil hates you. There is no distraction with him. He wants us. He wants you. You had better say NO!

One day I was counseling a young man. I was telling him that if he is going to be a man of God, his "No's" have to be convincing. When his coworkers asked him, "Are you going to the office party? There's going to be a little smoking, drinking, cussing, and other things there, but you don't have to." This is what this young man said: "I'm kind of busy that night." So what he said was, "Keep asking until I run out of excuses." God is saying, "Don't give the devil any excuses." Your answer ought to be: "I don't go to that." Your answer ought to be,

"I love God. I love Jesus. I'm not going there to mess around. I don't mess around so I'm not showing up." It's simple.

When we are really radical for Jesus, we bother people. We cause persecution. People say, "You're just a 'Goody Two-shoes,' aren't you? You think you're better than all of us." And you say, "No, I don't." "Yes you do. Every time you look at me, you're always looking down." "That's the Holy Spirit." "The Holy who?" "That's the Holy Spirit."

The powerful last-day Christian realizes that his or her family is being targeted by Satan. The focus of Satan is your family. Why? The family is the fabric of society. Without a family, you have no church. Without a family, you don't have the United States of America; you don't have a Canada, Singapore, Great Britain, or any country.

1.   Satan wants to steal the family. He wants fathers to think that their job is to bring home the bacon, make the money, and never pick up a vacuum cleaner for the house. You never do anything. You don't spend time with the kids, and then your kids are spiritual and social orphans. If fathers don't hug your daughters or sons, the gang member will. "Leroy" is waiting to take your daughter out.

2.   Satan wants to steal your finances. He would like everyone to be so broke that you can't do anything for God. He wants you so broke that not only can't you tithe, you can't even put five dollars in the offering. That's what he wants. Don't let him do that. Don't receive any condemnation. If you can't give ten percent, give two percent. I am just about the only preacher in America that

would say that! You do understand what I am saying? You need to experience the grace of God.

David went out from Ziklag and he attacked all of the Perezites and the other "ites." Remember, he attacked the Amalekites. Did he leave anyone alive? He killed them. He killed every woman, man, and child. By the way, before you judge God, it's his mercy that he didn't allow the children to grow up, die, and go to hell. You need to hear that before you shake your fist at God. There's only one God, and you are not him. Now, let's understand something. David went out and killed the people. Why didn't David reap the same thing? The passage says, "but they did not kill them."

3. They were spared by the grace of God. They were saved by the grace of God. But why? Why didn't he reap the harvest? Isn't the law of sowing and reaping powerful? Yes, but the law of sowing and reaping can be changed by intimate, powerful worship and praise. The law of sowing and reaping can be changed by powerful and radical obedience and running after God. Even though he killed, God spared his children. Have you ever sowed some wild oats in your life? I know I have!

Now you are concerned. The harvest is coming. Become a passionate worshiper. Become a passionate worshiper and radical obeyer, and God will change your harvest. The grace of God will come down upon you when you run after and radically obey God!

If you sow bad things, you are going to reap a bad harvest. I like to say, "except for the grace of God." David proved that: while he killed other people's wives and children, his own were spared. I think the key here is the grace of God. I like to describe the grace of God as two-fold: "unmerited favor" and "God's enabling power." Reading from Romans 5:17 in the English Standard Version: "If, because of one man's trespass, death reigned through that one man, much more will those who receive the abundance of grace and the free gift of righteousness reign in life through the one man Jesus Christ."

Reign—so the grace of God helps us to reign in this life. That enabling power of God can cancel some of the wild oats that we have sown before. The grace of God can actually prevent the reaping from past sins.

I don't know about you, but I was a very good sinner in the world. But now I am a very good saint in God. I obey God more passionately than how I obeyed the devil when I was in the world. When I sinned, I sinned. I was a good sinner. So be a good obeyer and obey God all the way.

4.   We must weep with brokenness and prophetic intercession for our family, the churches, and the nations. Not all is what it appears to be on Capitol Hill. Not everyone who says they are a Christian is a Christian. You need to understand that. I'm going to change the subject because God did not call me to be a politician. He called me to preach. God has a three-fold strategy. God is saying, "I want you to weep with brokenness. Not after the fact, but being proactive. Weep with brokenness now so you don't have to weep with brokenness later." What does God mean?

A. Continue in prayer and fasting. You have not because you pray not. You have not because you fast not. I ask people which prayer meeting they attend and they reply, "Oh, we don't go to prayer meeting." Well, no wonder you are messed up. How many hours or days did you fast? Fast? Let me say this in great love: Americans eat too much. You read that correctly. Let me write it Southern style: "Y'all eat too much!" Let me say it like a New Yorker: "Stop eating, bro!" We eat too much. Americans like hot dogs, hamburgers, drive-throughs, pull-through, and everything-through. Tribulation for Americans is when McDonald's runs out of Big Macs. There is no recession. The restaurants are full. Why? We love to eat!

Churches need to have corporate prayer meetings. At our church, there is an early morning prayer meeting three times a week. Every Tuesday we have one of the most dynamic prayer services any church could have.

B. As you are praying and fasting, you need to do vicarious repentance. Maybe you already know that vicarious means "substitutionary." Your son who is on drugs is not repenting. But, YOU can repent for him. You can act as if you are him. Say, "God, forgive my son Steve for getting high on crack. Forgive my daughter for living with a guy. Forgive them God. Forgive them. Lord, I vicariously repent for them. In Jesus' name."

I am starting to do this for the White House. Prayer and fasting isn't enough and vicarious repentance is not enough.

The Lord told me to tell you that we need to prophetically declare and decree over the problems and pains of your life and your nation.

We need to be able to say, "Lord, I speak and declare salvation over my entire household. I speak and declare salvation over my neighborhood. Salvation over this entire Wal-Mart. Salvation over this church." We need to declare it, say it, expect it, and believe it is going to happen. That's what the last-day Christian does!

THE PAIN

Now look at verse 6. The Bible says, "David was greatly distressed." Why? Because all of the people grabbed rocks and they wanted to kill him. These are David's close friends, but they have rocks in their hands. Have you ever told somebody, "You are a pain in the neck?" That's not what they were doing: David's followers were picking up rocks. Whenever people get distressed, they choose to attack the leader. If you are in leadership, expect it, get over it, and do what you were going to do anyway. People are going to attack you. It comes with the turf. I get attacked regularly. If it weren't for the grace of God, my wife and I would not survive.

The last-day Christian is an overcomer.

An overcomer is someone who can hurdle the obstacles in front of them. They are not defeated by problems. The overcomer welcomes trials and tribulations. He welcomes them because he realizes that tribulation is a blessing. Tribulation produces internal character in us. 2 Corinthians 4:18 tells us that we don't look at the things which are seen, but at the things that are not seen. The overcomer knows that the greatest lessons come from the pain of the experiences. During that time we are more humble, during that time we are more dependent on God, and during that time the grace of God (God's enabling power) helps us to climb over or endure the sufferings that we are going through at the moment.

Overcoming also means overcoming distresses or disappointments. The overcomer realizes what his focus has to be—he has to climb through hurdles, mountains, obstacles; he has to focus more on God's eternal purposes that He has for you rather than on the shortcomings of man. Forgiveness is not an option: it is a mainstay of an overcomer. Forgiveness enables you to bypass the shortcomings of man and focus on the wonders and the grace of God.

An overcomer learns that one really grows through the hard times, not the good times. You really grow during the painful times and not during the pleasurable times. If I were to ask you to give me three lessons learned during happy times, you would be hard pressed to do so. But you can probably give me ten lessons from when you were unemployed. You can give me twelve from when you had the flu. When someone was after you and talking behind your back, I guarantee that you were close to God. But when the happy times come, you learn nothing. You don't learn in the mountain. You learn through the valley experience. Most plants don't grow in the mountain, they grow in the valley.

The last-day powerful Christian overcomes distress. If someone is an athlete, they know this. If you are an athlete, you play like you practice. If you are namby-pamby in practice just because your finger got jammed, then you can't play, and you can't swing the bat. You will be namby-pamby when they need you, when the count is 3 and 2, the bases are loaded, and they need you to be a hitter. "My finger hurts." Your finger? Grow up already! You need to overcome personal distress.

2 Corinthians 4:16–18 says: "For the things which are seen are temporary. The things that are invisible are eternal." It's the invisible thing. God is working in you a far exceeding weight of glory. When you are hurting, that's where God wants you. Pain and hurt are the fertilizers of maturity.

So you ask, "Pastor, what about my past mistakes?" David had past mistakes. Welcome to the club called humanity. But no one drives looking in the rear-view mirror. If you drive looking in your rear-view mirror, you will run someone over. I'm tired of people who are driving this way. Please don't do that. Drive forward. Face forward. Forget the past. Put the past under the blood of Jesus. Suck it up and get going. Can you imagine if David had said, "Oh, please guys, after all I've done for you, please don't hurt me. Please don't hurt me. Put the rocks down." I wouldn't follow you if you cried to me like that. I would say, "Listen, I'll get my own wife. You can wallow in self-pity; I thought you were a man."

It's time for the men to be men. You are fighting real demons here. Weight lifting and washboard abs will not cut it. Physical exercise profits little; spiritual exercise profits much. (See 1 Timothy 4:8.)

The last-day Christian overcomes misunderstanding and attacks by those who are close to him or her, and those around him. Who are the people who were picking up rocks? People who were closest to David. A lot of people can take attacks from the outside; it's when it comes from the inside that they can't. It's like when David said, "Oh, I can take it from the enemy on the outside, but it was one who went to the house of God with me."

I want to prophesy something to you today. This is what the Lord says: "As it was with the first coming of Jesus when Mary and Joseph had a supernatural pregnancy, and were misunderstood and attacked by the people; yes, and even their family. The Lord would say to you that it should be the same way as we draw near to the Second Coming of Jesus. Many shall experience divine, supernatural pregnancies of visions and dreams and they shall be persecuted for it. They shall be attacked for them. They will have to overcome misunderstanding and rejection if they are going to go forward, says the Lord of Hosts."

THE PRAYER

1 Samuel 30:6b reads, "But David strengthened himself in the Lord his God." The powerful last-day Christian depends on God alone for strength and to see him through. He or she seeks personal encouragement and strength in his friendship with God. We love to sing Israel Haughton's song, "I Am a Friend of God," yet why don't we practice what we sing? Do you know what friendship with God means? It means you don't need people. I'm talking 2 Timothy, chapter 2 language. You are a soldier of God. You need to live to please Him who enlisted you. You need to be tough. How do you get tough?

You need to encourage yourself in God. Stop depending upon people. I'm not saying that we don't need friends, but we had better know how to survive without friends. You need to stop falling apart when you hold out your hand and someone walks right by you and doesn't even look at you. "Oh God, he didn't notice me." Get a life! There are people with great needs and some are committing suicide. We need to be soldiers in God. We need to encourage ourselves in the Lord. Stop complaining that "my church is not loving; nobody calls me." Call yourself! Look in the mirror. You are mighty in God. Hallelujah.

"None of the deacons call me. My deacon hasn't called me in a year." Well, when was the last time you called your deacon? "Pastor hasn't called me." When was the last time you called your pastor? Pastors and leaders need a lot of encouragement also. I'm not trying to be insensitive, but you need to encourage yourself in the Lord alone.

Psalm 62:5 says, "My soul, wait thou only upon the Lord; for my expectation is from him." You need to get this whether you are young in God or advanced in God. Expect everything from God and little from people, and you'll be fine. But if you expect a lot from people, they will let you down. Why? They are human just like you. Before you point that one finger, there are three fingers pointing back at you!

When the going gets tough, you need to toughen up in God. Don't give in to the following things when things get tough: self-pity, fear, and despair. Don't let these three things dominate your life and overwhelm you. Don't depend on people for your peace. Depend upon the Prince of Peace.

Discover the "peace that passes all human understanding!" (Philippians 4:6–7).

Write down these three P's: Pain, Poise, and Peace.

When you are in pain, you need poise. What is poise? Divine super-coolness. It gives you an attitude. "God is with me. The devil can't mess with me. You want some of this, devil? You really want some of this? I'm cool, calm and collected. Jesus lives in me!"

The other person is saying, "But you know, the pastor hasn't called you, and the deacon hasn't called, and the elders are watching you . . ." Would you put that violin of self-pity away, already! Put it away!

This attitude is the result of years of fellowship and intimacy with our heavenly Father. I don't mean to be cute. But instead of being into intimacy with God, most people are "into me, see." Everything is about them. If your ego is bigger than my church's dome, then we are bound to step on you sooner or later. Give it to Jesus! I have great advice for you. We are not that important; God is all important.

One time when we were in New York, a lady came to me and said, "This morning, the devil attacked me here; he caused the eggs to crack, etc." Everything was the devil did this, the devil did that. I said, "You know, ma'am, you must have a ministry greater than Billy Graham." She said, "What do you mean?" I said, "Because Billy Graham doesn't get attacked as much as you do." Three days later, she finally got it.

THE PARADIGM

A paradigm is a new model, a new strategy, and a new pattern. A paradigm is an innovative way of doing something. If you are in business today, what worked in 1999 is not working now. If you are saved today, what rescued you four years ago isn't going to rescue you now.

The last-day powerful Christian realizes it will take out-of-the-box leadership and bold new paradigms to rob the enemy. David was the unorthodox one. God is looking for unorthodox people. Unorthodox means you are not the same as everyone else. You are so different that the devil can't figure you out.

The devil sent Goliath, a big, nine-foot-tall giant with a huge spear, armor, and a look that would kill most people. All of Israel said, "My, look at him. He's so big, we are cooked!" Along comes David, who says, "I don't fight with swords and armor. I fight with a sling shot. That guy's head is so big. It's so big, how could I miss?"

Let me give a couple of prophetic thoughts:

1. David is the unorthodox one because he uses a sling-shot and a stone instead of a sword and armor to conquer Goliath. It's never been done until that time. God is looking for "It's never been done people!" This is what God is saying. God is raising a new generation of young-minded leadership to challenge and conquer present-day giants. He is raising up new people who are not afraid of the giants.

2. At MIT (Massachusetts Institute of Technology) in 1947, a professor of mathematics had the brightest mind ever recruited by MIT. He put an equation on the board. Over it, he wrote, "This problem cannot be solved." Then he told his students to solve it. Everyone beat their heads trying to solve it, but they couldn't. Forty-five minutes later, a little Chinese kid came in on a bike. He didn't realize it couldn't be done, so he solved it in five minutes. He came in with a new paradigm. No one told him it could not be done.

God is raising up teenagers today with spiked haircuts, tattoos all over the place, and they will kick hell out of the earth. They are crazy. They will do anything for God. I want to get behind them more.

Let me give you five things God is saying today about your daughter and your son. This is based upon 1 Samuel, chapter 17:

1. When you see a new leader, **recognize them**. In verse 31, Saul said, "Bring this kid to me. Bring David to me."

2. **Receive them**. All young people and parents know that my attitude towards youth is to receive them. Don't resent them. Don't resist them. Receive them. In verses 32–37, Saul says, "You are nothing but a kid." David said, "Sir, a bear tried messing with my sheep. I took him out. And when the lion showed up, I whacked him, too." That's the New Paradigm Translation. Recognize and receive them. You need to do this with your daughter and son. That weird son you think you have, he's a leader.

3. **Respect them**. Chapter 17:38–40. He says, "You come to me with a sword, but I come to you in the name of the Lord of Hosts and David ran toward him with his slingshot." This generation is going to run towards problems with new paradigms, new strategies, innovations, new creations, and they are going to whip the devil and drive him out!

This generation is trained to kill giants. Our generation was trained to coexist with them. Our generation is trained in how to keep talking about them. We talk about how big they are, and how shiny their armor is. These young kids will say, "Let's kill that dude. Let's move on. Just whack them and move on." Then we say "You can't kill that giant, you arrogant little kid," and they respond, "I may be arrogant, but I'm going to take on the giant and I'm going to whip him!"

4. **Release them**. We don't want to own our children. Verse 37 says, "Go, and the Lord be with you."

5. **Rejoice with them**. 1 Samuel 18:5 reads: "And David behaved himself wisely and whatever he did, he prospered." He did it with excellence. Then people started saying in verse 6: "Saul killed his thousands, but David killed his ten thousands." What old man Saul should have done is say, "You know what? That's my protégé. You are right; let's celebrate him." But instead, he became angry and jealous. He began to throw javelins at David.

We sometimes throw javelins at our young people. We kill their creativity because we've never done it that way before; we didn't look like they do. Well, maybe they don't look like us because they have to reach a generation that doesn't look like anything we know. This is a different generation. They want to read *Twilight* and about vampires and things like that. Do I agree with that? No. But the Lord is dealing with me.

I respect the young people. I respect that they are innovative and creative. They use computers like never before. I answer forty emails per day, but pretty soon I will have to get on Twitter, Facebook, and everything else because I need to talk to young people. I'm 60-ish, going on 39. I need to be able to talk to young people, to speak with the youth. I will talk to you if you're older. By the way, I talk to 23-year-olds; older people as well.

I talk to some older people and they haven't had a challenge in the last twenty years of their life. I don't have time for that. I don't have time to go back into the past. I am too busy climbing the mountains of the present and the future. That's the kind of pastor a church needs.

David and his men ate the showbread (1 Samuel 21:6). You weren't supposed to do that. In the temple there was a candlestick to light up, there was a table with bread on it, and only the priest could eat the bread, and if you were not a priest, you would drop dead. But David ate it because David understood the Spirit of the Lord and not the letter of the law. He knew that the Lord wanted true holiness.

With the rule to not eat the bread, God was trying to say this: "When you are holy, you can eat this physical bread and then you can eat my spiritual bread." David walked in and said, "Are you all hungry? Let's go eat the showbread. First, let's repent of every sin. Okay, you did. You got it? Good. It's lunchtime!" Do you know what? David did not die. He should have died, but he didn't.

David adjusts and adapts to change with creativity. In 1 Samuel 21:12–15 , the Philistines say, "Isn't that David, who killed Goliath and raided our people?" David knew that most cultures respect insane people; crazy people. So David begins salivating on his beard, making wild noises, and getting on all fours. Instead of dying, he adapts; he overcomes.

If you've done any training for the Special Forces or the Navy Seals, you know that whatever the problem, you improvise and you overcome. David improvised; he became a crazy man and winds up with the city of Ziklag. Hallelujah! But David lied. But I love his creativity. We need to be creative. "Pastor David, are you saying that we need to be crazy?" I am. I'm crazy for Jesus! I'm passionate and creative for Him!

David assumes apostolic authority in the presence of uncertain authority (see 1 Samuel 23:1–6 and 1 Samuel 30:7). That's why he takes the ephod. That's why he reads the Urim and the Thummin. The ephod was a vest. It had twelve stones for the twelve tribes of Israel on it. On the top right and the left, it had other stones called the Urim and the Thummin. We don't know exactly what those were, but basically, you would ask God something and either the voice of God would come to you or a voice would come out of the stones. We don't know, but you had to be a priest to do it.

So why didn't God strike David down? David is an Old Testament type of apostle. He walked in apostolic authority. The last-day powerful Christian will align himself with apostolic authority and have the victory.

THE PROMISE

I hear the Lord simply saying, "You shall surely overtake them." Do you want to take back what the devil stole from you? If you want to take back your family and finances, if you want to overcome distress and misunderstanding, if you are ready to seek God like never before, if you want to be out of the box, if you hear God saying, "Pursue for you shall surely overcome," please pray with me right now:

HEAVENLY FATHER, WE COME TO you right now in the name of Jesus. We come to you with an open heart. I confess that the devil has robbed me from my purposes in life. He has stolen from me finances, family, assignments from God; many things. But right now I ask for complete forgiveness.

SECOND, I AM DETERMINED TO pursue everything that you have for me. Give me the strength to do that. Allow your sustaining and enabling grace to give me the wisdom and the insight and the discernment to pursue and recapture everything that the enemy has stolen from me. Allow me to catapult forward and recapture everything that God wants me to achieve in these last days. Father, I confess that You are above the economy, You are above health issues. You are above my shortcomings. You and I are a majority. I can do all things through Christ who strengthens me. Therefore, I receive Your grace, I receive Your strength, and I receive Your discernment.

IN JESUS' NAME, AMEN.

CHAPTER THREE

GOD HAS A PROVISION FOR YOU

So David went, he and the six hundred men who were with him, and came to the brook Besor, where those stayed who were left behind. But David pursued, he and four hundred men; for two hundred stayed behind, who were so weary that they could not cross the brook Besor.

Then they found an Egyptian in the field, and brought him to David; and they gave him bread and he ate, and they let him drink water. And they gave him a piece of a cake of figs and two clusters of raisins. So when he had eaten, his strength came back to him; for he had eaten no bread nor drunk water for three days and three nights. Then David said to him, "To whom do you belong, and where are you from?"

And he said, "I am a young man from Egypt, servant of an Amalekite; and my master left me behind, because three days ago I fell sick. We made an invasion of the southern area of

the Cherethites, in the territory which belongs to Judah, and
of the southern area of Caleb; and we burned Ziklag with fire.

1 Samuel 30:9–14

Here is what God is saying: "It is time to aggressively take back all
the things the devil has stolen from you." It's time to take back the areas
where the devil has messed with you for long enough. When Jesus comes
back, He's not coming back for a weakling, beat-up, and defeated church.
He is coming back for a powerful church. Plan to be a part of that church.
He is not coming back for a half-defeated church waiting for a trumpet
to blow to rapture us out of here. We will be conquering, climbing, moving forward, and we have to advance. Now is the time!

Let me tell you a big secret. I'm so glad that people are scared of the
economic times in which we live. I'm glad they are thinking the world is
coming to an end; because it is. They need to think about God. We need
to be powerful Christians to reap them in.

THE PURSUIT

Mike Murdock says, "Pursuit is the proof of desire."[2] What you go
after tells me who you are. The Word says, "But David pursued." I need
to go back to the previous point where David prayed. If someone messed
with my wife Nellie and took my kids, I wouldn't want to pray; I would
want to go.

So I congratulate David. He controlled his emotions and asked the
Lord whether to pursue. Rule your emotions with discipline and prayer.
In these last days, emotionalism will not give you the victory. You can't
simply move out in anger. Besides that, which way do we go? The world
is a big place. The powerful last-day Christian pursues, with faith and
determination, what the enemy has taken captive.

---

[2] Mike Murdock, *The Wisdom Commentary* (Denton, TX: Wisdom International, 2001), 50.

I was at a restaurant the other day and my wife saw a big, beautiful, metal sign that said, "Faith" and I bought it for my desk. I intend to move in mountain-moving faith like never before. God does not respond to tears, pity, and needs. He responds to faith! Don't go to Him with all of that and then say you don't believe Him. Either the Bible is right or wrong, and I believe it is right. If you're going to be powerful, you need to claim the Bible. You need to speak the Bible. You need to think the Bible and you need to act on the Bible. If the devil has taken something from you, then get up, pray, and go after him in Jesus name!

Let me share with you ten things that you need to pursue and to recapture:

1. **Recapture your first love for Jesus.** Read Revelation 2:14–15. It says you have left your first love. You don't lose your first love: you leave it. How do you leave your first love? Through distractions. Through busyness. Through dealing with problems.

It happens every year just before Christmas, maybe even months before. Check out the store lines in the early morning hours the day after Thanksgiving! People go absolutely crazy. Do you line up to come to church? Would you spend hours to come to church? Would you spend hours at home waiting on God? No. But we will spend hours waiting for a store to open so we can mow someone down, knock over an old lady, in order to buy that item we need at a cheaper price! Recapture your first love for Jesus! Ask yourself every now and again: "Do I really love God with ALL of my heart?"

2. **Recapture your daily devotional time.** I had my devotions this morning. I had a wonderful time in God. I read four chapters of the Bible and all four chapters confirmed an important direction I needed for my life. If you are not having your time with God, ask Him for forgiveness. Just say, "Jesus, forgive me," and start tomorrow.

You might say, "But Pastor David, I work at nights. Good; then you can have your devotions at any time! Amen?

3. **Recapture giving your tithe and offerings first.** I didn't say not to buy anything. The country would go broke if we didn't buy anything. But don't you think you need to buy something for every person in your life? You are out of your mind. And don't charge it because maybe you are still paying for three Christmases ago. Be conservative. You can buy something for the baby and that's it. Don't go crazy! I will ask of you only one thing: radically recapture tithing and giving of offerings like you used to when you first got saved. I'm not trying to place condemnation on you. Some people are so broke they can't pay attention. Do you understand what I am talking about? If you can only afford to tithe two percent, then do two percent or three percent!

4. **Recapture the life of a manager, not an owner.** I have great news for you. You don't own anything. We own nothing. God owns it all. We are managers. Those of us who invest know what a money management account

is. When you go to a company such as E.F. Hutton, A.G. Edwards, and others, they manage your money and invest your money.

How would you like it if you went to get your money and the investment broker said, "Thank you for investing your last five thousand dollars; it paid for a cruise to Europe for me, my wife, and our kids!" You would want to hang him. It's against the law. You would tell him it's not his money: it's yours. That's how God feels each time we take His money and spend it for ourselves!

5. **Recapture the exercise of your spiritual gifts.** It's incredible what I'm about to tell you. Maybe you have the gift of prophecy. You used to prophesy. You used to move in the word of knowledge and the word of wisdom, but you stopped doing it. If you get a word of knowledge about someone wanting to commit suicide, you never tell anyone, and the church leadership is unaware that someone is going to leave church and commit suicide. I received a word of knowledge from someone about loneliness in the house, despair and suicide in the house of God. I called it out. Since I did, people were set free. Now imagine if those persons had kept it to themselves. I want to strongly encourage you to not keep your spiritual gifts to yourself. You need to practice your spiritual gifts in a small group setting or a Sunday School class. However, if you want to practice them in a church celebration service, your church leadership will judge it. We want spiritual gifts! We believe in the gifts.

6. **Recapture the obedience to witness and make disciples.** Acts 1:8 reads, "But you shall receive power after the Holy Spirit has come upon you. And you shall be witnesses . . ." The baptism of the Spirit is not to bless you. The baptism is not about just opening up the gifts of the Holy Spirit. It's to give you power and favor to talk to people about Jesus. We need to recapture that. Many have been baptized in the Spirit for twenty-five years. How many people have you witnessed to? Never mind leading them to Christ. Something is wrong when we have the ability to speak in tongues and we aren't talking about Jesus.

In Matthew 28:19–20, Jesus said to go out into all the world and make disciples. We need your witness and we need your testimony. We overcome the devil by the word of our testimony and the blood of the Lamb.

7. **Recapture your obedience to the two great commandments.** What are the two great commandments? In Matthew 22:37–39 it is very simple.

Commandment number one: You shall love the Lord your God with all your heart, soul, strength, and mind. The mind: how can you love the Lord with all of your mind? It means your predominant thinking for that day is about Jesus. Every now and again you might think about your kid in the hospital or the job that's going down. However, your predominant thinking is, "Do I love Jesus with all of my thinking?"

The second commandment is found in Matthew 22:39; it says, "You shall love your neighbor as yourself." James 2:8 says, "Follow the royal law. Love your neighbor as yourself and show no partiality."

Don't treat the rich guy better than the poor guy. Don't treat this guy better than that guy. Don't do that. Who's your neighbor? The person who lives with you. The people who are closest to you are your neighbors. In my case, my neighbors are Pastor Nellie and my dog Buddy. Those are my neighbors. But then I also have people who live near me.

Your neighbors are your Christian brothers and sisters. We should love each other more than anyone else. When you visit your family for the holidays, do you have some of "that kind" of brother and some of "that kind" of sisters? When they say, "Come here and give me a hug," do you say, "I'm in for it now." Or that aunt who's always bringing up when you were three years old and did certain things. She says the wrong things right in front of everyone. Of all the ones you have to introduce, you really don't want to introduce these, but they are there. Do you have those types of family members?

We don't choose our family. You don't choose your brothers and sisters in Christ, but you have to love us. You have to be crazy about us. How do you treat your family? You treat them great. You provide for their needs. You don't talk behind their back. You don't tear them down. The only thing you should try and say about them is something good. Remember Ephesians 4:29, "Let no corrupt word proceed out of your mouth, but what is good for necessary edification, that it may impart grace to the hearers."

8. **Recapture the pursuit of eternal rewards.** I want you to be in heaven with me. That's my life's mission:

for YOU to be in heaven. Secondly, for you to not only be in heaven, but also to have a great life in heaven. I want you to live in a great-looking house or mansion in heaven. I want you to have a nice-looking front yard in heaven. I want you to have a custom-made car. The things you do here affect the way you live everything else. But you've got to recapture your pursuit of the eternal and your eternal rewards. You have to think about eternity every day. Think about it every single day. He is coming very soon!

9. **Recapture Kingdom order in our relationships.** What do I mean by Kingdom order? I mean Bible order. The head of every house is the husband; and husbands need to take their place. Don't be an Ahab. Husbands need to be involved in the discipline and the planning of their home. Their job is not just to bring home the money. Their job is to help rule the house along with their wife as their equal and their joint heir.

The husband's job is to love his wife, and die for her if necessary. That means dying to his feelings and his opinions. The wife is to submit to her husband, respect him, and not fight him at every turn. The children are to be in submission to the parents. All of these new television programs are all wrong. Shows like "Family Guy" all make parents look stupid and the young people look smart. Let me tell you something: that is not the Kingdom. Remember, what you put in your eye-gate comes out of your mouth and into your thinking.

10. **Recapture the apostolic order in the church and over your life.** 1 Corinthians 12:28 reads: "And God has appointed these gifts in the church." Then Paul numbers the gifts. "First: apostles, second: prophets, third: teachers, fourth: the working of miracles, five: gifts of healing, sixth: helps, seven: administration, and eight: variety of tongues." They are listed in this order for a reason and the church has to get back to the Bible's order. It is amazing that there are denominations, even in the faith movement, that do not accept the apostle and prophet. They accept the pastor, teachers, and evangelists, but the others have died away. That's just as bad as some of the evangelicals who don't believe in any of them.

I didn't say this, but God said this. First, the apostles. I say this tenderly and gently . . . but we have churches that are dominated by the lesser gifts, particularly the gift of administration. Administrators are your trusted counselors. You can't have a church without administrators. We need them. Visionaries need administrators, but please note they are listed as number seven, not number one. I am called in an apostolic gift and I function in my local church as the lead pastor. You need to understand that when you align your life under the apostolic, you will have order in your life.

I am not attacking or knocking anyone. I am teaching the way things are to be in the church. Don't let me become your enemy simply because I write the truth.

THE PERCEPTION

We need to be people who perceive well. In 1 Samuel 30:10 it says that a lot of David's men became: "so weary." I want you to get the picture. God says to go. David has six hundred men with him. They start chasing the enemy, and they get to a river called the Besor, and two hundred of the men said, "We can't go on with you, David. We are so tired. We are exhausted." I can imagine the other guys saying, "Man, you guys are a bunch of chumps. They took our wives and you're getting to sit here saying you're tired." The others respond, "I know, but I just can't go on anymore." I want to speak prophetically by saying that a lot of us are tired; a lot of us are weary. When fatigue comes in, faith goes out. That's why Jesus says, "You have to come apart and rest for a while." So David says, in verse 24, "Okay, you two hundred stay here and guard the supplies. The rest of us will go and attack the enemy."

When they had the victory, David said, "Everybody gets an equal share of the reward." The other men said, "Wait a minute, these guys didn't do anything. They were so tired, they couldn't even move across. They ought to be happy with getting their wives and cattle back." David said, "No. On the day of victory the team all shares together." There is a great lesson in this. The powerful last-day Christian responds in compassion and sensitivity to the needs of those close to him or her. We need to respond with compassion and sensitivity.

Ever since I have been born again, I have had an all-consuming passion for people to go to Heaven and not to Hell. It has been the number-one motivating factor of my life. It has been, not an obsession, but a burden. I have learned that I am required to view people as someone whom Jesus died for—even people I don't like. Jesus died for that person. This is someone Jesus died for.

Then, when I heard John Bevere's study *Driven by Eternity,* it added a second burden to me. Not only am I concerned about people going to heaven, but now I am concerned about people getting the eternal rewards that they should be getting, because we are going to be spending more time in eternity than we are here on the earth. So I am concerned that, first of all they get to heaven, and, second, that they get their rewards when they get there. I came to that realization around 2010 when I did that study by John Bevere.

Here is how John Bevere challenges the last-day Christian:

> Let's not miss our assignment! It's time, the season is upon us, and He's at the door! If we don't fulfill our destiny, then God will have to raise up another generation like He did with Joshua's to complete His house, for he has already decreed that His house will be full.

> All it takes is us doing our part and multiplying what He's entrusted to us. Don't be discouraged. Don't see your part as insignificant. Don't lose your passion. Don't lose sight of the heavenly vision made clear in the New Testament . . . Not only are others in your generation counting on you— some are in desperate need for you to reveal to them Jesus, others are in need for you to extend His encouragement and strength—but your eternal destiny awaits you. You can succeed by utterly depending on His grace. He is faithful![3]

---

[3] John Bevere, *Driven by Eternity* (New York: Faith Words, 2006), 259.

I want to share with you eight keys to loving leadership.

1. People's needs are more important than a project achieved. People are more important than numbers. People are more important than the bottom line. People's needs are more important than things. The people who work with me are more important than the things in my life. Your son is not a "thing"—he is a person. In a house, people are more important than your accomplishments. As a supervisor or a boss, if you look out for the needs of your people, they will forever be loyal to you. Their productivity will increase by 300 to 400 percent. But if you drive them and think about the bottom line only, you will eventually lose not only productivity, you will lose your people.

2. People need to be led by motivation and modeling rather than by being driven. No one likes to be driven. "Come on, man or woman, we have a deadline. We have a deadline!" No one likes that. You can feel pressure well up in your throat and in your heart, and who can work in a situation like that? I do realize that some people need to be motivated, but you will get much more productivity using motivation instead of intimidation. David could have easily said, "You two hundred are chumps; just go back. If we find your wife, we will bring her back. If not, tough on you." He didn't say that. Instead he gave them a job.

He told them to guard the supply lines, which is in the rear. While the two hundred guarded the supplies, if the enemy tried to flank them from the rear, they were the rear guard. They protected the army. So it's not as if they didn't do anything.

3. *How* we get somewhere is just as important as getting there. People say that the end justifies the means. No, it doesn't! Just because you achieve building a building or a church and you run over people in the process, that's not God. What good is achieving a project if you lose 300 to 400 people in the process? There are losses in every war and battle, but you don't have to do it on purpose. How do we get there? Getting there with the fruit of the Spirit and with the love of Jesus is just as important as getting there.

4. All contributions, no matter how small, are vital to the team's accomplishments. Think of David's two hundred men. If you are supervisor or a business person, speak "Team" to your people. Let them take ownership of it. We are a team. That's why in the secular world we see teams wearing the same shirt. I went to a business the other day and they were all wearing hockey shirts with their names on the back of the shirt. I thought it was cool. The Holy Spirit told me, "They are a team. You need to tell the church that they have to be a team." As Christians, we are a team of friends. We work together. We don't work against

each other. We are all important. I can't do anything without my staff, trustees, elders, and lay leaders in my church. Forget it. I did not build this church. The Holy Spirit is building it through His people!

5. Delegate wisely. David was smart and he was led by the Lord. He was always in prayer. The Lord told him to take the two hundred, let them guard the supplies, and let them be your rear guard. If you are a manager, write this down. Don't dump—delegate. What is the difference between dumping and delegating? When I dump on you, I give you a task to do without providing direction, timelines, or accountability. When I delegate to you, I explain what my expectations are, I tell you when I want it, and I will check up on you every now and then. I will give you enough water to turn the canoe. Do you understand? But if I am dumping on you, I think I am delegating, but I'm not, because I am not giving any direction. People who get dumped on usually don't last long. The church is notorious for dumping on people.

6. Avoid exhaustion. Every now and again we all get tired. If we work hard, we get tired. But God is not calling you to burnout and exhaustion. In 1 Kings 18, Elijah is the champion and in 1 Kings 19 he is the chicken. He went from champion to chicken in one chapter. He was completely exhausted.

You must eat right, exercise right, and rest right. You have to plan hobbies. Everything my wife Nellie and I do is for this moment. Everything we do. If I go on vacation, it's so I can do my task right. It is like my hand stretching a rubber band. I stretch it back and forth, again and again. No one can stay in a stretched position. You must un-stretch. How do you un-stretch? Ask the Holy Spirit to give you a hobby. Ask Him to give you a diversion. Make it something that you enjoy. Make sure it is something that will re-energize you. What's the word? Recreation. You need to recreate. But if you keep stretching and stretching you will eventually snap. The first thing you will take it out on are those close to you and who love you.

7. Don't allow strife and division on your team. The men told King David, "Are you going to give those vaga- bonds a part of the spoils?" David said, "Yes, this is a day of victory, and we will divide the spoils equally. What they did is just as important as what you did." If you are over an organization or a business, never ever allow strife and division to continue for long.

Pride tends to elevate itself by looking at the deficiencies in oth- ers. Pride likes to point the finger downward and say, "You did noth- ing, so I can puff myself up as if I really did something." We tend to judge others by their faults, but we judge ourselves by our intentions! "Yes, but I didn't mean it." Forget that; why are you willing to cut your- self some slack, but not others?

8. Team Celebration. I'm starting to move more and more into this. If we lose, the leader should take the blame. If

we win, we share the credit with everyone. We need to celebrate and celebrate more.

THE PROVIDENCE

David's army found an Egyptian. Please let me paraphrase. In verse 1 of 1 Samuel 30, David took three days to get to Ziklag. On the third day, when they got to Ziklag, when they were getting closer, they smelled smoke. When they got there, the place was burned down. They said it was over.

Maybe you are saying that your situation is over. But I want to prophesy to you today, that three days earlier, after their enemies burned Ziklag, God arranged for an Egyptian boy to get sick.

Instead of taking the boy with them, the enemy had to leave him in a field. In the three days that it took David to get there, an Egyptian boy was there waiting for them, and he was the plan to show David how to get his property back. Do you know what God is saying? There is an Egyptian waiting for you to run into him. Hallelujah! Three days before they even knew that there would be misery and destruction, God already had a way of escape. God had an answer. "But Pastor Garcia, it's a big place?" What are the chances of four hundred guys running into this kid lying in field? With God, you have a great chance of finding him. Let's look at the providence of God.

The name of the capital city of Rhode Island is beautiful: Providence, Rhode Island. Providence means sovereignty. Providence means it's all in God's hands. Providence means for the people of God, that you are in God's hands, that nothing can ever happen to you except you are in God's hands. People ask, "Who's in control of the world? God can't be because there is so much misery." Well, the devil isn't, because no one would get saved or healed. God is in control of the people who are in covenant with Him.

The powerful last-day Christian expects supernatural intervention because he or she is in covenant with God.

Supernatural intervention means when God invades our situation and through His enabling and sustaining grace provides us with money, gives us healing, or more important, gives us favor with people, so that all of a sudden those who were against us are now for us. The money we didn't have, we now have; the health that was failing is not failing; we are healed.

Supernatural intervention simply means when God comes, either through His angels or His mighty Holy Spirit, situations turn around.

Let's examine four insights. These four insights can literally change your life.

1.   Faith in the miraculous belongs to the decisive. The first word in verse 11 is the word *then*. What does *then* really mean? *Then* after they started marching. You will never get an answer until you get moving in a direction. Some of us want all the directions, all the understanding, all the clarity, all the T's crossed and all of the I's dotted before we move one blessed inch.

But if you have all of the answers, the answer is wrong. If you have all of the things lined up, it's not the will of God. God does everything by faith. He will always leave an amount of unknown, in order to see if you trust Him. Do you understand that concept? Stop trying to say, "God, this missions trip that's coming up: my heart's saying yes, but my mind is saying I don't have any money. I don't have this, that, and the other." Oh Jesus, no! Learn to be decisive!

Opportunity is always where you are, not where you were. We have to find and take inventory of what we have going for ourselves. What do I have in my hand? God asked Moses in Exodus 4, "What do you have in your hand?" Moses had a staff. This speaks of what positive things are happening in my life right now. What positive things can I utilize to achieve what God wants me to achieve? Instead of focusing on the negative, what I don't have, we are to focus on what is positive. The positive is whatever momentum is happening in our life that we can ride on to victory.

Find out what is going good in your life right now. Utilize the gifts you do have—do not focus or be distracted by what you are lacking—focus on what you have and run with that.

David could have said, "What are we going to do? We lost this and we lost that." Opportunity is not where you were; it's where you are. Get up and do something!

John L. Mason said this: "Each of us has the ability to create what we need from something that is already here."[4]

Get up. You've got to do something. You must get moving. "But Lord, I need You to provide that." Well, do something for the Lord to provide. What do you have? Elisha asked the widow in 2 Kings 4, "What do you have?" She said, "I have a jar of oil." "That's all I need," Elisha said. She kept pouring and pouring until all her needs were met.

Teddy Roosevelt said, "Do what you can with what you have, where you are."[5]

---

[4] John L. Mason, *Conquering An Enemy Called Average* (Tulsa, OK: Insight International, 1996), 29.
[5] As cited on Brainy Quote, accessed May 4, 2014, http://www.brainyquote.com/quotes/authors/t/theodore_roosevelt.html

Edward Everett Hale said, "I cannot do everything, but I can do something. I will not let what I cannot do interfere with what I can do."[6]

There are two ways of looking at a gas tank. It's either one-quarter full or three-fourths empty. I'd rather say it's one-quarter full than to say I'm running out of gas.

God always involves us in the miraculous. God could have told David to step aside, sent a battalion of angels to kill the Amalekites, pick up their families, drop them back in Ziklag, wave His hand, and rebuild the city. God always involves us. When feeding the 5,000, He used the disciples to set the people down in rows. The giving is God's. But the taking is ours. God gives you His promises, but you need to take His promises.

Someone in business might say, "I'm still working for someone, but God, You said I would have my own company." Yes, but what are you doing to take it? Be faithful and fruitful in what is another man's and God will promote you (Luke 16:12). Walk in humility and in the fear of the Lord and you will have riches, honor, and life (Proverbs 22:4).

2. Revelation is progressively revealed. When did they find the Egyptian? On the way to where God told them to go. Would they have found the Egyptian if they sat around? How did David know which way to go? God probably told him to go that way: "Go down to the brook named Besor." Can you imagine if they had sat there saying, "Which way did they go, George, which

---

[6] As cited on Brainy Quote, accessed April 2, 2014, http://www.brainyquote.com/quotes/quotes/e/edwardever393297.html.

way did they go? No, I want to go that way!" Or saying, "I want to put it to a vote." Had they voted on it, they all would have died. Do you understand what I'm saying? Someone had to take the initiative, and then they found the Egyptian. As you move forward in life, more instructions will come.

If anyone has ears to hear, let him hear. Then He said to them, "Take heed what you hear. With the same measure you use, it will be measured to you; and to you who hear, more will be given. For whoever has, to him more will be given; but whoever does not have, even what he has will be taken away from him."

Mark 4:23–25

Therefore take heed how you hear. For whoever has, to him more will be given; and whoever does not have, even what he seems to have will be taken from him.

Luke 8:18

As you move forward, more information and more revelation will be given to you.

3. The promises of God are always backed by the sovereignty of God. What do I mean by sovereignty? I'm talking about the power of God . . . the promises of God . . . the providence of God. I'm talking about the presence of God. God's promises are always backed by

His presence. David and his men are walking, and they smell smoke. They get closer the second day, and then they see smoke. They get there on the third day, and Ziklag was all in ruins. Do you think it was a coincidence that three days before that, after their enemies had burned Ziklag, the Amalekites were running away and the Egyptian guy says, "Can you all slow down a bit, I'm a bit tired?" They say, "If you can't keep up, we need to leave you here." Remember, the Amalekites were cruel. They left the kid there with no water and no food. They didn't leave him even a knapsack. If they had left him with a knapsack, he would have eaten some food and then gone the other way. But no, he stayed there. God worked it out that he stayed there. God provided an Egyptian at the moment David went there, and suddenly they all knew the enemy's battle plan.

You know what God is telling you right now: there's an Egyptian that's already been planted in your path—the path of obedience. There is an Egyptian and a provision for you, and you are about to walk into it. Your promise is coming. Your victory is on its way. It's guaranteed. God doesn't love David more than He loves you. There is an Egyptian, a provision, waiting for you.

There are seven kinds of "Egyptian" provisions:

1. You are walking in life, looking for a job, and God gives you favor. What does that mean? It means **divine, preferential treatment**. You don't have the grade point average that someone else has. But you apply to a college and amazingly they not only

accept you, they also give you a full scholarship. Do you want to know why? It's because you have divine, preferential treatment in your life! You bid on a contract and others bid lower than you, but you get the contract because you give to missions, and you give to God! Therefore, God gave you the contract.

2. **Coincidences or God-incidences.** Say that word: coincidence. Did you ever say, "Something funny is going on here?" This is something God showed me. Every time you run into a "coincidence," it was an Egyptian that God wanted you to run into.

3. **Confirmations.** God often uses my wife and other sources to confirm His will to me while I'm in the process of preparing my sermons. Let's say I'm writing something on obedience. Suddenly, on the television or in a song my wife is playing, I will hear a word about obedience. It's amazing. Or someone will email me the exact scripture that I was writing; not just reading it, I will be writing it. That's why I come in like a lion with confirmations.

4. **Unexpected blessings.** I could tell you stories upon stories about unexpected blessings. You've seen the advertisements on television about claiming uncollected state or federal funds. Some people do not collect funds that are owed to them. I want to challenge you to write your agency and give them your name and social security number, and ask if they have anything

for you. I know; it sounds preposterous. But it wouldn't surprise me if they say, "Yes, we have been looking for you. You have $173,889.53!" When you get it, you must declare, "Hallelujah; I'm going to tithe!" And don't forget about supporting missionaries who are going out in Jesus's name. What do you have to lose? You might say, "No, that won't happen to me." Stop being so pessimistic; . . . unexpected blessings can be yours!

5. **Angels.** Hebrews 11:4 says, "Angels are ministering spirits." Our Father is the father of all spirits. Hebrews 13:2 says, "We have entertained angels unawares." Let me tell you something: you have talked to angels. I guarantee it. Maybe that guy with the sign that says, "Will work for food," or "I'm hungry," and you say, "This man is ripping people off. He's just an old wino!" You might have just passed by an angel and just failed your test. I'm telling you that you have entertained angels unawares. Angels are God's Egyptians waiting for you to have a need.

6. **Sovereign interruptions.** Have you ever been interrupted and you say, "Of all the times for there to be a knock at the door!" That knock at the door might be an Egyptian in disguise. Your flat tire might lead to closing a business deal. Are you with me? You are changing your tire, and someone stops to help you, and that person needs to hear your testimony. You've been saying

to God, "Use me." Well, here's your chance; don't throw it away in a sea of complaining.

7. **Sovereign interventions.** All of a sudden, God begins to invade the situation, and He plants an Egyptian three days before David had a need. The Holy Spirit is saying to you right now: "I have already provided for you, even before you ask for it."

CHAPTER FOUR

TAKE BACK WHAT THE DEVIL HAS STOLEN FROM YOU

Our key verses are found in 1 Samuel 30:15-31:

And David said to him, "Can you take me down to this troop?"

So he said, "Swear to me by God that you will neither kill me nor deliver me into the hands of my master, and I will take you down to this troop."

And when he had brought him down, there they were, spread out over all the land, eating and drinking and dancing, because of all the great spoil which they had taken from the land of the Philistines and from the land of Judah. Then David attacked them from twilight until the evening of the next day. Not a man of them escaped, except four hundred young men who rode on camels and fled. So David recovered all that the Amalekites had carried away, and David rescued his two wives. And nothing of theirs was lacking, either small or great, sons or daughters, spoil or anything which they had taken from them; David recovered all.

Then David took all the flocks and herds they had driven before those other livestock, and said, "This is David's spoil."

Now David came to the two hundred men who had been so weary that they could not follow David, whom they also had made to stay at the brook Besor. So they went out to meet David and to meet the people who were with him. And when David came near the people, he greeted them. Then all the wicked and worthless men of those who went with David answered and said,

"Because they did not go with us, we will not give them any of the spoil that we have recovered, except for every man's wife and children, that they may lead them away and depart."

But David said, "My brethren, you shall not do so with what the LORD has given us, who has preserved us and delivered into our hand the troop that came against us. For who will heed you in this matter? But as his part is who goes down to the battle, so shall his part be who stays by the supplies; they shall share alike."

So it was, from that day forward; he made it a statute and an ordinance for Israel to this day.

Now when David came to Ziklag, he sent some of the spoil to the elders of Judah, to his friends, saying, "Here is a present for you from the spoil of the enemies of the LORD" – to those who were in Bethel, those who were in Ramoth of the South, those who were in Jattir, those who were in Aroer, those who were in Siphmoth, those who were in Eshtemoa, those who were in Rachal, those who were in the cities of the Jerahmeelites, those who were in the cities of the Kenites, those who were in Hormah, those who were in Chorashan, those who were in Athach, those who were in Hebron, and to all the places where David himself and his men were accustomed to rove.

Some things are not of God.

1 Thessalonians 5:5–6 reads: "You are all sons [and daughters] of light. And sons [and daughters] of the day. We are not of the night or of darkness. Therefore, let us not sleep, as others do, but let us watch and be sober."

Anything that has animals turning into humans or humans turning into animals is satanic. Like the Harry Potter stories, the movie *New Moon* also emphasizes this. I would like to share a quote from Ed Young, Jr., who said, "We are humanizing animals and animalizing humans."[7]

That's what's happening right now. Vampire movies are denigrating, making a mockery of the blood of Jesus. You need to understand Acts 15:29, where it says to abstain from blood. We are able to live forever because of the precious blood of Jesus, not human or animal blood. The movie *New Moon* (I read this, as I have no intention of

---

[7] Ed Young, Jr., from a 2009 television sermon.

seeing it) depicts people who live for hundreds of years due to their drinking human or animal blood. Beloved, we do not live for hundreds of years. It is appointed for man to die once. You are not going to be a vampire because you draw physical, emotional, or sexual energy from someone. You are going to die! I want to lovingly tell you that in the *Twilight* series, the humans make a covenant with the wolves that they will not suck human blood; that's all demonic.

Cosmetic dentists are now making a fortune by charging 1,000 dollars a pop for people to get fangs. Yes, you read that correctly: fangs. People are exploiting modern-day vampires. The devil has you hooked reading books, but it doesn't stop there. There are people who are so demonized that they are living vampires now. I'm talking about lawyers, doctors, police officers, etc. They actually feed off physical and emotional energy, nature, sex, and blood. No, not every modern day vampire sucks literal blood, but some of them do.

You will become demon-possessed if you pursue these things. Parents, you are not your teenager's friend. Be a father and a mother. Get rid of those things. You are bringing demons into your homes. I realize that I might be ruffling some feathers by saying this, but I am writing this in love. Please understand my heart. How would you feel about a doctor who finds a tumor in your body, but his attitude is, "Gee, I really don't want to hurt her feelings, so I will let her leave with that tumor. She will be dead in six months, but she will die happy." I'm not that kind of doctor. I am a soul doctor. I am here to teach life, so that you may have life abundantly. But don't condemn teenagers and singles when they are attracted by these things: they are simply being drawn to relationships and friendships that the church should be providing.

When we see teenagers who look a little weird, hug on them and love them. Ask their names; make them feel like they are very important, because they are very important.

We have already looked at 1 Samuel 30:1–17. I want to prepare you to know that God wants you to take back everything the devil has stolen from you. 1 Samuel 30 is a picture of the Christian in the last days. He's not perfect. David has made mistakes. As a matter of fact, he robbed the Amalekites first, and now they are getting him back. Have you, like me, ever done anything wrong? Maybe you are paying for it. But we live by the mercy and grace of God. This passage is a picture of you. It's a picture of me. We might get knocked down, but we won't stay down. We are going to get up and take back everything the enemy has stolen.

David was greatly distressed, for the people spoke of stoning him, because the soul of all the people was grieved, every man for his sons and his daughters. But David strengthened himself in the Lord his God. Then David said to Abiathar the priest, Ahimelech's son, "Please bring the ephod here to me." The ephod was their way of knowing whether one had heard the voice of God or not.

Abiathar brought the ephod to David. David inquired of the Lord saying, "Shall I pursue this troop? Shall I overtake them?" He answered him, "Pursue, for you shall surely overtake them and without fail recover all." I want you to know that God doesn't want you to get some of it back or most of it back, but ALL of it back!

We've already studied how God supplied an Egyptian kid who got sick. The Amalekites left him without a canteen of water or food. They left him to die.

I can imagine this Egyptian kid's thoughts. If he believed in anything, he was calling on whomever he believed in. "God, if you are there, do something, or else I am dead meat." It just so happened that when David and his men started going, they bumped into this Egyptian. Because of this Egyptian, they were able to find out where the enemy was and take back everything.

Maybe the devil has stolen from you. Maybe you are in foreclosure; maybe you are in bankruptcy; maybe you have cancer. But I'm here to tell you that there is an Egyptian ordained by God to lead you into the victory. Even though you messed up, the mercy and grace of God is here to help you take it all back!

THE PASSION

If you are going to take back what the devil has taken, you must have passion. If you are in the military, you must have passion. If you are going to war, you better have passion. You don't fight without passion. If you fight with fear, you have lost already. So David leans over and says, "Can you take me to them?"

The powerful last-day Christian is enthusiastic about taking back all from the enemy. Say in agreement with me, "Enthusiastic!" It's not about taking some or most back, but everything! The devil has robbed a lot of people of revelation. You might be saying, "I married the wrong person." If you did, you are stuck. You can't give her or him back. That's not what I'm talking about. I am talking about being enthusiastic about taking back what the devil has stolen from you.

The word *enthusiastic* comes from the Greek *entheous*, which literally means "in God." Why? The people who were in God were people who were passionately excited. That will take a week to sink in! If you are in God, you should be a passionate person. Now you may have to send a text message or make a telephone call to your face to let the rest of us know about it. But I want you to know that you should be a passionate person.

Please understand that you will not be remembered for your good intentions; you will be remembered for your passions. I recently did a funeral where everyone talked about how much the deceased love horses. "Oh, how she loved animals." "Oh, she loved children. She lived for children." What will you be remembered for? Will they say, "Oh, he was a God-lover. She was a God-chaser. I'm telling you, she loved God!"

Let me share a few concepts about passion.

1. Passion is the enthusiasm that provides strength for the task. Why? Passion is your moral and physical strength. You have more moral and physical strength when you believe and are excited about what you are doing. When you are excited about what you're doing, it gives you strength. When you are excited about what you are doing, your heart pounds more. When you are excited, you have more adrenaline. Ecclesiastes 9:10 in the New International Version says, "Whatever your hands find to do, do it with all of your might." Why? In the grave, where you are going, there is neither working, nor planning, nor knowledge, nor wisdom. While you are alive, whatever you do, do it with gusto! Do it with all of your heart!

Joy is critical to enthusiasm. Joy is absolutely critical. You must have joy. I did not say hilarity. I didn't say you wake up and are laughing. That's not what I wrote. That's not joy. Joy is quiet peace in the face of suffering. Joy is confidence that God will see you through.

Nehemiah 8:10 says, "The joy of the Lord is my strength." In John 16:22, Jesus says, "No one can steal your joy." Did you understand that? The devil cannot steal your joy! No one can take your joy. Your girlfriend or boyfriend breaking up with you cannot take your joy. Your house in foreclosure cannot take your joy. We surrender our joy. We give up our joy. No one can take our joy. We make a decision to surrender it. What happens to us? Circumstances happen, time goes by, and we surrender our joy. But passion is the enthusiasm that provides strength for the task.

2.   Passion is the result of being shaped and motivated by what we love. You will be remembered for what you love. What you love is being shaped by the passion you have and your passion is being shaped by the love you have.

John L. Mason said, "If you ignore what you are passionate about, you ignore a part of your potential that God put inside you."[8]

Write down this scripture, Proverbs 27:19: "As in water, a man's face is revealed. So a man's heart reveals the man." That's my paraphrase. Just as water reflects the face of a man, his heart or his passion reveals who that man is. What's in your wallet? What passion do you have? What are the top three things that your closest friends would say about you?

I hope they say, "What a great passion for God he has." I hope they say, "what a passion to obey and serve Him, and to win souls with her

---

[8] John L. Mason, *You're Born an Original—Don't Die a Copy* (Tulsa, OK: Insight International, 1993), 15.

giftedness." Your passion gives you away. Your passion lets everyone know what you want in life.

In Matthew 22:37, Jesus says, "You shall love the Lord your God with all your heart, with all your soul, and with all your mind." You know what He was saying: you need to have passion for God . . . with all you've got.

3. When you add passion and emotion to belief, it will become conviction. You must be driven by passion and conviction. John L. Mason also says, "You can do anything you want with your life except give up on something you care about."[9] Do you know that it's impossible to give up on something you truly love and care about? For example, you will never give up on your children.

I remember about three Christmases ago: a homeless man came into the church. Behind him was a beautiful German shepherd: dirty, but beautiful. The man told me it was cold outside and asked if I could I get him a place to stay. I told him I would. I didn't check with anyone else. I phoned the local hotels and told them that so and so was coming, and then he asked me, "What about my dog?" I told him that the hotel would not take his dog. He said, "If the dog can't go, neither will I." The Holy Spirit spoke to me because, sadly, I was not able to help him. The Holy Spirit said, "You see how this man is passionate about his dog? That's how your people need to be about Me!" I never forgot that. He said, "Where my dog goes, I go. Where I go, my

---

[9] Ibid., 15.

dog goes." I pray that every young person would say, "Where the Holy Spirit goes, I'll go. Where He doesn't go, I don't want to go!"

Dr. Mike Murdock decrees this: "What generates passion and zeal in you is the clue to revealing your destiny. What you love is a clue to something you contain inside of you."[10]

That's why I listen to young people who love baseball, or ballet. Maybe you are called to be a dancer for Christ. You only need to surrender your passion to the Lord.

THE POISE

This Egyptian kid wasn't a dummy. This kid says, "Wait a minute, if I tell them where they are, I am dead meat. This guy is going to whack me. He will take me out." So he says, "Swear to me by God that you will neither kill me or deliver me to the hands of my master, and I will take you down to this troop." He was slick; that's what we call poise.

What is another word for poise? Composure. This Egyptian was cool, calm, and collected. The powerful last-day Christian is cool under pressure. He's composed under pressure.

What is poise? Whatever you do, you keep your emotions under control. That doesn't mean that when you respond to the Spirit, you lift one hand and put out less energy than a car. I am talking about a quiet confidence in God during times of adversity. Why do I say this? I believe that life has a way of not cooperating with us. I believe that we expect some things and most times other things come up.

I believe life is like a baseball game. Sometimes curve balls are pitched at us. We swing and miss. When this happens, don't

---

[10] Murdock, Mike, *The Wisdom Commentary*, Wisdom International, Denton, Texas, 2001.

conclude that you are not to play in the game anymore. Stay in the batter's box of life, keep swinging, and you are bound to hit it out of the park. You need to stay in the batter's box and keep swinging. You need to remain composed. You need to remain poised. You don't need to listen to voices saying, "It's all over now." How many times have you heard, "It's all over," yet you are still here?" Look at you. You are still here!

Poise is not the same as accepting your present temporary situation as your future permanent situation.

Let's say you file bankruptcy, and not too many people know about it, but God knows. If you file bankruptcy, it's not your permanent future. Even with a bad credit rating, your credit rating one day will be okay. If you are divorced today, guess what? There is life after divorce. I am not endorsing divorce, but I am lifting up those friends who have been divorced.

There's life after being a widow. I know you said, "I cannot live without him or her." But what's temporary now doesn't have to become permanent!

God is a God of provision. If you are in foreclosure now, guess what? God has a lot more houses for you. God has a lot more things for you.

"But pastor, I've been diagnosed with cancer and I have only three months to live and my situation is all messed up." It all depends upon how you look at it. Not to be insensitive, but if you die, you step from this temporal body into an eternal body, and you begin to live in the presence of God. You don't die. You move into a better situation.

Poise is realizing that for every problem you face, God has a scripture and a response. God has a Bible verse. As a matter of fact, He probably has five Bible verses for every situation you face. Or He has a response. What do I mean by that? I mean that He has a personal word for you that will speak, or whisper, to you, saying, "Don't you worry about it. It's going to get better." "How will it get better, Lord?" That's not for you to know right now. It is going to get better!

THE POSITIONING

The scripture says, "*There* they were." Let's read verse 16: "And when he had brought him down, there they were, spread out over all the land, eating and drinking and dancing, because of all the great spoil which they had taken from the land of the Philistines and from the land of Judah." Did the enemy have any guards up? No. Were they concentrating on defending their perimeter and position? No. How were they positioned? Spread out all over the place. What were they doing? They were drunk, partying, and careless. Verse 16 is for you. God positioned them into a ripe, fat turkey for the pickings, by magnifying (amplifying) three things that were inherently inside of them. He magnified their carelessness, their carousing, and their carnality.

Carelessness: they didn't have any guards. They were all spread out. Anyone in the military knows that you should concentrate your forces. You set up a perimeter. You put up shields. But no: they were overconfident. They were thinking, "We've got it made. We're the man. We're so bad. No one can whip us." When you get proud, huffy and puffy, the devil will slap you down.

They were carousing. They were drinking: drunk as a skunk. People ask, "What's wrong with drinking?" The dangers of carousing. That's what's wrong with it. You can't have the Holy Spirit working in your life and have your body filled with drugs and alcohol at the same time. You can't be vigilant in the Spirit when you are intoxicated in the natural.

They were also carnal. The implication in the Hebrew is that they were doing all kinds of things. How many men did David have with him? He had 400 men. Two hundred were too tired and so he took 400. He took 400 against overwhelming odds. How do I know that? Four hundred young men, who were smart, used the technology of the day and rode away on camels. In our time, we would say they used their laptops to get away.

They were up against uneven odds. David attacked and whipped them without losing a single man. Why? Because they were careless, carousing, and carnal. Therefore, make sure you don't become careless, or the devil will come into your house and take your daughter. He will take your son, your virtue, take your virginity, your job, and everything else.

We don't need to be carousing when we go to work. We need to be the best employees we are capable of being. Don't roller skate into work tomorrow morning. Get there wide awake and ask God to use you to bless your boss and bless the company. Don't roller skate in with a *"cum si cum sa"* attitude and complain like everyone else. If so, you deserve to be fired. Make yourself "fireproof." Make them have a board meeting and say, "Whatever we do, we have to keep her (or him) on. He (or she) is too good!"

Here is a word to the wise. You don't want to be like the Amalekites were in verse 16. You don't want to be all spread out. You don't want your family going this and that way. You want your family to be in unity. You want your family concentrated and praying every night. If the devil shows up, we want to rebuke him together in the name of Jesus.

The powerful last-day Christian expects God to give him or her the victory. You expect it. You look for it. You plan for it and you act like it. How? Those who are obedient should expect God to prepare them and position their circumstances for victory. The disobedient need not apply. You will cause weakness in your defense if you move in rebellion, if you can't submit it to authority, or are always sassing your teacher and your parents. You cannot expect any blessings from God. If you are always conniving and planning to usurp the pastor's authority in the church, God will never bless you. I'm writing to people who plan on being obedient. I didn't say perfect. I said in your heart, your obedience should expect God to prepare you. "But pastor, King David was disobedient in the past. David did stupid and silly things." Yes, but in his heart, David was a man after God's heart.

I am saying that there is grace for you!

Be a man or woman after God's own heart.

Go after God. You will make mistakes along the way. But you will also reap the Egyptians along the way, because your heart desires to serve and be a blessing to God.

Psalm 37:23–24 reads, "The steps of a good man or woman are ordered by the Lord. And he delights in his [or her] ways. Though he [or she] falls, they will not utterly be cast down, the Lord upholds him with his hand." How do I know who the godly are? They always come back.

THE POSITIVENESS

In verse 17a, it says that David attacked them. The powerful last-day Christian attacks the enemy's stronghold with confidence and optimism. When you attack, you attack. That's why some elite soldiers say, *"Curah,"* they will attack. World War II parachutists jumped out of the plane yelling, "Geronimo." You need to attack. In the martial arts, they are ready to fight. They don't go, "Huh?" Our troops in Iraq don't say, "Yo, we are coming down the road, please clear out the mines and please don't hurt us." If you fight like a punk, you will wind up a punk. Do you understand what I am saying?

It's time for the tough to get going. We are not punks. We are not the tail. We are called to be the head. We are called to snatch victory from the jaws of defeat. Say out loud: "Confidence! Optimism!" Send a message to your face. The next time you face the devil, be confident and optimistic. Jesus purchased not only our salvation, but also our joy and victory.

1 Corinthians 15:57 says, "Thanks be to God who always causes us to triumph in Christ Jesus." What are our weapons? Here are some old-fashioned weapons that were good back then and are still good right now. They get better and better.

1. The first weapon is the blood of Jesus. We need to take the blood of Jesus with us. People ask, "You believe in that stuff?" I sure do. His blood not only saves, it sanctifies and it protects. It's the best covering you need. If you have an alarm system in your house, cover it in the blood of Jesus. We need the blood of Jesus as our weapon.

2. The second weapon is the name of Jesus. There is a name that's above every name. The Bible tells us that it's a name to which every knee will bow: in heaven,

on earth, and even under the earth. Every demon will bow down to the name of Jesus. Cancer has to bow to the name of Jesus. Poverty has to bow to the name of Jesus. Forgetting your homework has to bow to the name of Jesus. Hallelujah! Are you getting excited, yet? (Of course if you didn't study, you will need a lot more than just the name of Jesus!)

3.   The cross of Jesus. Stay next to the cross. It was the cross that obtained our victory. We don't preach a gospel of modernism and self-help. We preach a crucified Christ, a blood-shed price, and a resurrecting Christ. He had to die to give us the victory. That cross tells us that we have to die on it as well.

Galatians 6:14 tells us: "As for me, God forbid that I should boast about anything except the cross of our Lord Jesus Christ. Because of that cross, my interest in all the attractive things of the world was killed long ago, and the world's interest in me is also long dead" (NLT).

4.   The Word of God. Take the Bible with you. The Bible is a great weapon. Use the Bible. Don't just read it. Memorize it. Don't just memorize it. Speak it. Don't just speak it. Believe it. Don't just believe it. Expect from it!

Bible patterns bring Bible results. Read Hebrews 4:12.

5.   Our Testimony. The Word divides between soul and spirit, but our testimony is Revelation 12:11: "They overcame by the blood of the lamb and the word of their testimony.

A few weeks ago in my church, a young man got up and said, "I don't think I can make it." The Holy Spirit led me to say, "Everyone who has ever been on drugs, come up and encourage him." There were about fifty people who came up to the altar. They all said the same thing, "I did it. I did it." I saw him recently and he is doing well!

Keep your testimony right. Keep talking. Keep believing. You might say, "Pastor, if I tell everyone that I am saved and sanctified, I might have to live it." That's the idea! We have to live what we say. We have to say what we live and believe.

6. The anointing of the Holy Spirit. The anointing is a special touch (or enablement) from the Holy Spirit for a specific task. You have an anointing. Read 1 John 2:20 and 27. Verse 20 says, "You have an unction from the Holy One." You have an anointing from the Holy One. You don't need to be taught the anointing. You have it. That anointing is not just for the well-known evangelists. That anointing is not just for David Garcia. That anointing belongs to YOU! You need to realize and use it. You need to wield it and expect results from it. The anointing in your life will remove burdens and destroy strongholds in people who are bound and struggling (Isaiah 10:27; Luke 4:18–20). A fifteen-year-old kid who realizes that when the anointing comes, burdens roll away and strongholds are destroyed. You need to believe that.

7. The armor of God. Ephesians 6:11–18 is a great portion of scripture to encourage us. You might think that armor

is only for defense, but that's not correct. The sword is not only defensive, it's also offensive. The shield was not only defensive. Soldiers also fought with their shield. They fought with their helmets. They fought with their belts. We need to use these weapons!

If you want to be confident and optimistic, never take advice from your fears. Why? Your fear is going to tell you, "You need to think this over. You are not capable." I can do all things through Christ who strengthens me. Maybe you are living in worry; you need to crucify that worry and give it over to Jesus.

If God demands all the glory, you will never get the answers before you go. If God wants all of the credit, then you will have only partial revelation and partial instructions before you go. He wants to see if you will take a step on His directions of "Go!" He is not going to prove Himself to you until you take that step of faith.

When we were leaving the States to be missionaries in Zimbabwe, all of our friends in New York City asked if I was taking our six-year-old daughter and wife over there to be murdered. There is violence in Zimbabwe. But did you forget that we lived in the South Bronx? Do you realize that there are more murders in the Bronx than in Zimbabwe? Get behind me, Satan. God will never give you all the revelation before you move forward.

God has an "Egyptian" for you and for me. Glory to God! Praise His name. If He can do it for me, He can do it for you. You've got to go before you can understand. Some of us have never gone on to do much for God, because we demand to know all the answers before we take a step. But the Word says that the just shall live by faith, not logic or reasoning. If you understood it all, then why would you need God? You wouldn't need to obey God. You wouldn't need to agree with Him.

God will always multiply steps of faith, but He cannot bless fear and indecision. I am reminded of the four lepers in 2 Kings 7:3–7. I am reminded that the enemy, the Syrians, had surrounded Jerusalem and were starving the people. We pick it up in verse 3.

> Now there were four men with leprosy at the entrance of the city gate. They said to each other, "Why stay here until we die? If we say, 'We'll go into the city'—the famine is there, and we will die. And if we stay here, we will die. So let's go over to the camp of the Syrians and surrender. If they spare us, we live; if they kill us; then we die." At dusk they got up and went to the camp of the Syrians. When they reached the edge of the camp, not a man was there, for the Lord had caused the Syrians to hear the sound of chariots and horses and a great army, so that they said to one another, "Look, the king of Israel has hired the Hittite and Egyptian kings to attack us!"

The enemy got up and fled in the dusk, and abandoned their tents and their horses and donkeys. The Hebrew implies that they dropped everything and ran with the clothes they had on; they abandoned their food, fires, tents, horses, and donkeys. "They left the camp as it was and ran for their lives."

When you begin to take a step of faith, God sets an ambush for the devil. When you get up and begin to move forward, the provision and the miraculous comes. If you want to live in the realm of the miraculous, you'll never have all the answers. You will never be powerful within yourself. You will have to lean on God, believe God, and God will see you through. Bless His precious name!

Realize that there is a thin line between optimism and pessimism. The thin line is your outlook and your attitude. The way we see things is the way we attack them. The way we see our wife is the way we treat her. Allow the Word of God to pierce and saturate your attitude, in Jesus' name.

I bless you today with a renewed passion for your assignment; a new passion to serve God, a renewed passion for business, a renewed passion to study. I call you enthusiastic. I call you to have strength for the task. I call you to be shaped and motivated by love. I call you an outstanding person. You are a person motivated by your love. I call you a person of conviction. I call you a person of poise, with a quiet confidence in the day of adversity.

I declare today that you will not accept your present, temporary situation as your future permanent situation. I pray that you will let God create your world, because man will always make it too small. I speak that, for every problem, you will realize that God has ten scriptures and ten responses. I position you for victory and to take back what the devil has robbed from you. I speak that you are a person of victory! I speak that you are an overcomer and that you are filled with the Holy Spirit.

I speak obedience. Not some, not half, but fully obedient to the Lord. I declare over you right now that you are a positive person, filled with faith and confidence and optimism, and that you will never take advice from your fears, ever again. You will never hang out at the complaint counter of life and you will never develop negative thinking in the dark room of worry. You will take steps of faith even though you don't understand all of the answers. I speak that you will know that you know that God is there to give you the victory. I speak that as you move forward, God will multiply and multiply your efforts. For every step you take, God will take 10,000 with you. I speak anointed eyes for a godly outlook and an anointed mind for a godly attitude. If you receive these things, shout to God right now and say, "God, I receive these things!" In the name of Jesus!

CHAPTER FIVE

PERSISTENCE AND WISDOM BRINGS PROMOTION AND VICTORY

We are still looking at 1 Samuel 30:15–31.

PERSISTENCE

Victory will belong only to the persistent. You need to be persistent in the last days. You need to get up and decide to take back everything the devil has robbed from you! Do not rest until you get it all back. God is making provision for you to get it back. The powerful last-day Christian does not stop until he or she recovers all. Say: "Recovers all!"

God is not saying to take some of it back or most of it back. God is saying to take all of it back, and then some.

You can be "cool" under the pressures of your daily life! Deuteronomy 33:25 gives a great promise: "As your days, so shall your strength be." According to the pressure and the challenges of the day, you will have spiritual strength and spiritual insight.

1. You can keep your cool by expecting the strength of the Lord.

2. You can keep your cool by focusing. The number one cause of failure is focusing. We have to keep our focus.

3. Paul says, "This one thing I do . . . " You can keep your cool by focusing on the things that you need to, and not letting yourself be distracted to the left or the right until you achieve those one or two things.

4. You need to look at every challenge in front of you as something that God has allowed you to have. If God allowed it, God will see you through.

We see this in Mark 4:35–41. Jesus told the disciples, "Let's cross over to the other side." That was his command. After the command, they had a crisis—a storm arose. The crisis was the windstorm. The disciples said, "Jesus, don't you care?" Jesus wakes up and brings calm. You can be cool under pressure when you realize that every command is followed by a crisis.

If God gave you the command, it is up to God to see you through to the other side. "He who calls you is faithful, who also will do it." (1 Thessalonians 5:24). How do you respond to difficult circumstances? If you will remain calm and cool, yet persistent, you will be victorious. Remembering "Command; crisis; calm" will make the difference in your life—you can be cool under pressure.

Not only can you be cool under pressure, but you can recover ALL that the devil has stolen from you! That's what the Lord is saying.

Unfortunately, you have probably already lost something to the enemy, so let me share with you three insights about recovering all.

1. You must know that what was taken was legally yours. Beloved, if you're saved, you are in covenant with God! The devil has no legal grounds to rob, steal, and destroy. He has no legal grounds to ransack your home. He has no legal grounds to take your money. He has no legal grounds to take your health. He has no legal grounds to hold onto your unsaved daughter or unsaved son. They are coming home! He or she is going to get saved. But you have to know that these things do not legally belong to the devil. You have to know this because you might say, "Well, my daughter deserved it." No one deserves to go to hell!

2. You are scripturally entitled to seven times more. Meditate on Proverbs 6:30–31: "People do not despise a thief if he steals to satisfy himself if he is starving. Yet, when he is found he must restore seven-fold." When the enemy robs you, he must give you back what is due, plus interest.

3. You must not stop until you get it all back and then some.

I want to share eight insights about persistence and success. Calvin Coolidge said, "Nothing in the world can take the place of persistence. Talent will not. Nothing is more common than unsuccessful men with talent. Genius won't do it; unrewarded genius is almost a proverb. Education will not; the world is full of educated derelicts. Persistence alone is omnipotent."[11]

I really like what the famous football coach, Lou Holtz, said about persistence. "Persistence is, in my mind, the quality that is most critical to success and happiness. Nothing takes the place of persistence."[12]

Persistence helps you to have true compassion for others in need. We have to say, "God, show me a need in their life and let me be there to fulfill it." Tell them, "If you ever need something, I will be available to you." Secondly, do good works to them. If they are in the hospital, mow the grass for them, or have it mowed; have your lawn service to mow theirs as well. Do good works; be there to provide a need for them. Third, be open and transparent to them. Say, "I want to see you to become born again. If you ever have any questions, I will be glad to answer them for you, but I will not pressure you."

Live by James 3:17: "But the wisdom that is from above is first pure, then peaceable, gentle, willing to yield, full of mercy and good fruits, without partiality and without hypocrisy." Gentle here means to be considerate. Follow this rule, "God leads . . . the devil pushes."

Let's look at six insights about persistence and success. If you are in business, a father, in college, people will pay money for this information.

1. Victory will always come to the most persistent. The difference between winners and losers is that winners hang on a little longer. Don't be a loser, and don't be a quitter.

---

[11] As cited in Dictionary.com, accessed on April 2, 2014, http://quotes.dictionary.com/Calvin Coolidge.
[12] Lou Holtz, *Wins, Losses, and Lessons* (New York: HarperCollins, 2006), 57.

2. "It takes time to succeed." Success is the natural reward of taking time to do anything well." – Joseph Ross[13]

3. John L. Mason said, "No one finds life worth living. You must make it worth living."[14]

Your life is worth living. We must not allow the urge to quit win over us. You have to meet it, greet it, and defeat it. You have to keep on going. Don't roll over and die in negativity and defeat. If it's going to be, you'd better do it. Don't wait for someone else to do it. Don't wait for a political party to do it. In the name of Jesus, grab on to God, go get it, and make it happen.

4. John L. Mason also said, "Persistent people always have this attitude, they never lose the game, they just run out of time."[15]

Do you understand what I am saying?

5. Most people never succeed in the long run, because they quit due to either sustained adversity or boredom. I remember when the Holy Spirit spoke that to me. People stop the intensity of their marriage and say, "Well, she ought to know I love her." No, Bubba, you bought her romantic cards when you were dating, keep buying those cards now! "Well, I have her." What makes you think you have her? You need to love that woman. You need to keep loving that woman. Don't trust the enemy. Keep that persistence going. Your marriage is

---

[13] John L. Mason, *Imitation Is Limitation* (Bloomington, MN: Bethany House, 2004), 32.
[14] Ibid., 32.
[15] John L. Mason, *Know Your Limits, Then Ignore Them* (Tulsa, OK: Insight International, 1999), 47.

not on cruise control; it's always shifting. If you pick up the clutch too soon, it will clog on you. You will go home one day and she won't be there. Then you will say the devil took her. The devil didn't take her:, you gave her to him.

6.   It is conviction, not commitment, that perseveres in spite of time passing and in the face of adversity. We do not need to be people of commitment. We need to be people of covenant and conviction.

Conviction is embracing spiritual truths in spite of adversity and boredom, and before they are fulfilled.

You need to hang in there. I love what Winston Churchill said, "Bulldogs are so ugly, they are cute."[16] He said that the nose of the bulldog is slanted backwards so he can continue to breathe without letting go. We need to have bulldog tenacity. Keep breathing while you hang on. I am not going to let go of my daughter until she is saved. I'm not letting go of my friend until he is saved. I'm not letting go of this business until it prospers. I'm not letting go of Jesus.

Be a bulldog and grab hold of God. Don't let go!

Aesop, the Greek storyteller, said, "When it's all said and done, as a rule, more is said than done."[17]

A lot of people talk the talk, but never walk the walk. The other day, I watched a documentary on ESPN, and the Holy Spirit focused my eyes. It was an interview with the most successful basketball coach in American college history, John Wooden. John Wooden was

---

[16] Winston Churchill, as cited on Famous Quotes, accessed on April 2, 2014, http://www.all-famous-quotes.com/Winston_Churchill_quotes.html.

[17] As cited on BrainyQuote, accessed February 13, 2014, http://www.brainyquote.com/quotes/quotes/a/aesop118961.html.

a motivational speaker even in his 90s. He coached UCLA for 28 years. He won more national titles than anyone else. And he was married to his wife Nellie for 53 years. He continuously, persistently, told her how much he loved her. He would tell her every day, continuously, through-out the day. Nellie died on March 21, 1985. One interviewer asked, "Coach Wooden, you've been doing something strange ever since then?" He answered, "Yes. I write Nellie a love letter every day of every month since she died. I love you that way, honey." (Speaking to his wife.)

You need to be persistent. Don't let the devil take your wife. You might say, "I'm not affectionate, that's not me." You had better be-come like that! You are fighting demons. Don't think your honey is always going to be waiting for you if you remain abusive and unaf-fectionate. It doesn't work that way.

PRUDENCE

Prudence is not a name. Prudence means wisdom (see vv. 18–20). Do you want to know what the wisdom of God is? David recovered all; that's the wisdom of God. We are in a bad economy right now, but you will get it back and then some. That's what your attitude should be. You have to go out there saying, "I'm going to get it back. I'm under God's economy, not the world's."

The powerful last-day Christian exercises wisdom and sensitivity in dealing with his or her fellow Christians. In getting it all, don't run over people. In getting it all, treat your employees right. If I have to run over the little guy while getting it all, I am not walking in the Spirit. If I have to hurt you to achieve, I am not walking in the Spirit. David saw that there were 200 guys who were tired and could not move. He left them to guard the supply lines. David took 400 with him. They were outnumbered, outgunned, and they whipped the enemy. The 400 said, "Don't tell us you are going to give what we captured to those guys," referring to the 200. "They did nothing, man!" That's like when teenagers say, "I did all the work and you're going to give them an allowance?" All of a sudden, David said, "No. It can't be that way. The man who guards the supplies and the man who fights will have an equal share."

"How do I become sensitive? How do I walk in prudence and wisdom?" you might ask.

Wisdom is knowledge. But more important than knowledge, wisdom is insight. It's a wise attitude or course of action. To paraphrase Proverbs 24:3, "a house is built by three things: knowledge, wisdom, and understanding." Knowledge is the accumulation of facts, wisdom is the application of facts, but understanding is the arrangement of those facts. I can't apply wisdom unless I understand the strategy involved with the facts.

Proverbs 4:7 says: "Wisdom is the principal thing; therefore get wisdom." Wisdom is the foundation for all of our decisions. To quote Mike Murdock, "We don't really have a problem except a wisdom problem. We don't really have a marriage problem: we have a wisdom problem concerning marriage. I believe wisdom is the master key to everything we have in life."[18]

The fear of the Lord is the beginning of wisdom (Proverbs 9:10). Here is how you walk in prudence and in wisdom:

1. You must be able to see the entire picture. Never allow your children to say, "But Johnny got this; why can't I get it? Why can't I get what they have?" You cannot

---

[18] Mike Murdock, 2009 "Wisdom Keys" television program, Daystar Television Network.

have what they have because that's not what God is saying. You need to see the whole picture. Parents, ask God
for wisdom, especially if you have more than one child.
Ask God, because you can't treat each child the same.
Ask God, "What do you have for this son that you don't
have for that daughter? What does this worker have
that that one doesn't have?" We need anointed wisdom
and prudence in our leadership.

2. You are sensitive to the weak and exhausted. If you are
    not careful, you can look down on people who didn't
    have what you have, so they can't do what you can do. If
    you aren't careful, you can almost look down at some-
    one and say, "Man, get out of the gutter. You need to do
    this and that." There will always be weak people. There
    will always be tired people. Let's love them. Let's pick
    them up. Let's enable them and not alienate them.

To paraphrase Hebrews 12:12–13: "Strengthen the hands that hang
down, lest they become dislocated." There are too many dislocated
Christians. There are too many Christians who are "de-churched." All
they seem to talk about is how much they were mistreated in church.
We must love them back. They don't need any preaching. They need
you to tell them, "It's a new day. You need to go back to church and
give us what you have and we will give you what we have. But you
must forgive."

3. You make win-win decisions. This is especially true
    if you are a manager. A win-win decision is one that
    blesses you and is good for everyone on the team.

Everyone gets a win out of it. "But I deserve more," you say. It's okay. You might not have gotten more. But he who deserves nothing got something. He got something, she got something, and we all grow up together.

We need to say, "I need to make win-win decisions for my home. I've got to make win-win decisions for my team. I have to make win-win decisions for the company I work for." In the church, we have to make win-win decisions. Many times, that means swallowing our pride. Swallowing is what you might deserve. In John 3:30, John the Baptist says, "I must decrease so that He (Jesus) might increase." For you to get bigger, I may have to become smaller, and that's okay. As long as you win, that's all that matters.

PROSPERITY

1 Samuel 30:26 says, "Now when David came to Ziklag, he sent some of the spoil to the elders of Judah, to his friends, saying, 'Here is a present for you.'" This is amazing! I want to ask you a question. Does the text say that God told him to do it? No, it says that David wanted to do it. The powerful last-day Christian is extra-generous in evangelism and missions. As a matter of fact, the Holy Spirit does not have to say anything. You just want to give. We spoke of the gift of love. There is one particular family I am burdened for, whom I will not name. They have multiple children, and I am looking for someone to partner with me in my church so we can bless this precious family.

1.   David's offering was beyond what was required. It was above tithes and offerings. David felt like giving a blessing to the tribes of Israel. This is when you are led by the

Spirit of the Lord. You are beyond the Holy Spirit telling you to give. There are times the Holy Spirit doesn't say to give and you want to give anyway. Have you ever blessed your family members even though God didn't tell you to bless them? You love them so much, you just blessed them anyway. This is what I am writing about. We are the family of God. We live in blessing.

2. David gave because he wanted to, not that he was led to by God. It is my desire to see you super blessed! To see you in eternity with crowns is my desire. That is my particular desire.

3. Prosperity should lead us to generosity.

PROMOTION

Get ready to receive powerful truths. Let me describe to you what happened. In 2 Samuel 1, King Saul is killed in battle. He is mortally wounded, so he tells his armorbearer to strike him dead. His armorbearer says he cannot do it. Along comes an Amalekite. Saul tells the Amalekite to strike him dead, and he agrees. He also plans to bring some of Saul's belongings to King David, with the hope of getting some money. The Amalekite goes to King David and says, "Saul is dead." David asks, "How do you know?" He said, "This is his armor and this is his sword." David then asks, "How is it that you did not fear God when you struck and touched the anointed of God?" Then David has the Amalekite killed.

Read 2 Samuel 2:1-7. David becomes the King of Judah. As soon as he does, in verses 8-32, there is a civil war. New levels do bring new devils. Promotion is coming to the powerful last-day Christian. The powerful last-day Christians will function as kings and priests. Did you know you are a king? Do you know you are a queen? Did you know you are a priest?

Revelation 1:6 says, "And [He] has made us kings and priests to His God and Father, to Him be glory and dominion forever and ever. Amen." A king rules, so we just don't overcome, we don't just barely make it with losses and some gains—we rule. We are called to be leaders and not just followers. Romans 5:17 tells us, "We are destined to reign." We are not ruled by circumstances: we are above circumstances. Spiritually speaking, we are in a higher, exalted position. Ephesians 2:6 tells us that we are seated in the high heavenly places.

So we rule in the sense that although we are physically here on the earth, spiritually we are above the circumstances, not under the circumstances. 2 Corinthians 4:16–18 says that while we suffer things here, they are working in us far more exceeding glory, an eternal glory. We are rulers because Christ is being formed in us every single moment of every day. We are rulers when problems seem to be overwhelming. We are not just called to survive and go through them. We are called to rule in the sense because we've learned the eternal lessons. We have applied the principles of the Word of God and we have leaned on God's everlasting strength.

Revelation 1:6 says we don't survive, we rule! We don't survive, we kick the enemy aside. When the rapture comes, we don't say, "Oh God, what took You so long? Bless God; You are finally here!" No, you say, "Jesus, come. Hallelujah!" God is calling us to overcome and rule where we are.

1.   We are spiritually promoted to a greater kingship and rulership.

Saul is killed in 2 Samuel chapter 1. This means that whatever has oppressed you for years is about to go away. Saul's day is coming. God will promote and bless the obedient person who never touches the Lord's anointed. Isn't it interesting that David had two opportunities to kill Saul, but he resisted the temptation. The first time, Saul is hunting David. In 1 Samuel 24:1–22, David cuts a piece of Saul's robe and tells Saul that he could have killed him, but he didn't. The second time, he takes Saul's spear and a jug of water while he was asleep (1 Samuel 26:7–25).

What does this mean to us? It means to be careful that you don't try to move an authority from his or her assigned position. Be careful, my friend. Your pastor is God's anointed. If you cannot support him or his vision, then leave in peace, but don't cause strife and division. God will bless you and promote you if you are obedient and never mess with the anointed. Your teachers and your bosses are the anointed. The same goes for whether you are in the church or in the workplace.

You may not like the president, but he is still the Lord's anointed. I pray for him often. Those are the ones who will be promoted. You cannot rule if you are touching the ruler. If you don't understand this and it's too heavy for you, pray for understanding.

2. We experience a greater level of warfare. Make a serious note of the following. Look at 2 Samuel 2:8–32. The minute David is promoted, his own son, Ish-Bosheth crowns himself the king over Israel and there is a civil war. When new levels bring new devils, new anointing and new rulership brings division from those who don't want kingdom principles.

Be careful that in the things God is doing, we don't begin fighting one another. Be careful. We don't need to fight each other in the home, church, or anywhere else.

3. We exercise rulership in prophetic prayer and worship. What is prophetic prayer? Instead of saying, "Oh God . . ." and giving Him our petition, or "Oh God, You know I am hurting and please answer this . . . " These prayers are called supplications.

But when you are a ruler, when you are a queen, when you are a Debra, you prophesy that prayer. "I declare in the Name of Jesus, Church, what are you doing sick? In the mighty Name of Jesus, line yourself up. I speak death to this cancer in the Name of Jesus!" You begin to prophesy prayer. You begin to declare it. You are not asking; you are saying it. You have to tell the devil to get out of the way, because he doesn't want to move.

4. We rule by casting out demons and principalities corporately. I see an authority over demons that I haven't seen since Africa. We will simply touch people and demons will begin manifesting.

We don't challenge principalities. They are ruling angels, not demons. Angels don't fly. There are ruling angels over each country. You do not have to challenge them alone. But you can challenge them as a church. That's the secret. Kingdom people exercise rulership over territories.

5. We bring Kingdom influence to our work, schools, neighborhoods, and to our church. Wherever we go, people will notice that we are different.

CHAPTER SIX

ENCOURAGEMENT FOR LAST-DAY CHRISTIANS

I want you to read this one verse; 1 Samuel 30:6. "Now David was greatly distressed, for the people spoke of stoning him because the soul of all the people was grieved, every man for his sons and daughters; but David strengthened himself [or encouraged himself] in the Lord his God."

I want to give you ten words to encourage yourself in the Lord. Say that: "Ten words for encouraging myself in the Lord." If you read all of 1 Samuel 30, David, through compromise, had gone to the king: that was Goliath's king. He was afraid of being with Saul and so he went and pretended to be crazy. The king took him in and gave him a city called Ziklag. Ziklag means "winding" or "confusion." That's David's headquarters; can you imagine? David would go out and raid all of the Hitites, the Perezites, and the Amorites and all of the other parasites. He would just go out and raid. He would come back and the king would say, "Did you have a good raid today?" "Oh, we killed a lot of the king's enemies," and the king thought he was talking about the Jews. But he wasn't killing the Jews, he was killing the king's allies.

When you live a duplicit life, what goes around is going to come back around to you. So one day while he was out on a raid, the Amalekites came, and they burned Ziklag. As we have already read, David saw all the smoke going up. There is nothing more terrifying than to know your wife and your children are back there, and to realize that they have all been killed. David left no witnesses alive, and you know the law of sowing and reaping. So David is thinking that the Amalekites have killed everybody. He goes back there and sees that they didn't kill everybody, and he realizes that they took them hostage.

David had two wives at the time. That should tell you something. They took them both hostage, so all the men started weeping in the camp. Imagine your eight-year old daughter, your two-year old son, the baby: everybody's gone. When people go through grief, part of grief is that you get angry. So David's men pick up rocks, and they look at David. They are about to stone him. You need a word from God when your followers are about to stone you.

The Bible says that David strengthened and encouraged himself in the Lord. I believe he prayed. I believe he did a lot of the things we are going to see here, but not all at once. Friends are wonderful. If you have more than two friends, you are very blessed. If you tell me that you have ten real, true friends, you're probably kidding yourself. I'm talking about a real close friend; somebody who would die for you and do anything for you. There are different levels of friendship. Friends are wonderful, relatives are wonderful—we all need somebody to talk to. But there comes a time when God will allow you to have no one. You'll try and call the pastor and he will be out of the country or not available. Or the line is busy; or "I lost my cell phone." It's God, many times, trying to teach us something. Maybe the Lord is saying to you: "You need to plug into Me, instead of trying to run to the pastor or one of the elders." It's time to grow up!

When your daughter is twelve years old, you expect her to call you. But when your daughter is thirty-two, you don't expect her to call you and say, "Mom, we ran out of milk." "What are you calling me for? You're a grown woman." Wouldn't we tell her that? Wouldn't we tell our son, "You need a ride to the cleaners? Dude, you need to get your own ride; you're married now. You have your own family." We've trained them to not need us.

We were made in the image of God. He is training us to not need people, but to always need Him. You have got to learn how to encourage yourself in the Lord. I want to warn you, if you don't learn this lesson, you're going to have a lot of false guilt and you're going to have a lot of false conflicts. God will purposely cut people off from your life until you learn how to stand on our own two feet.

You have got to gird up your loins. What does that mean? You have got to be determined that you are never going to leave God. You are always going to serve God. You are not going to be down in the dumps. You are going to stand on the joy of the Lord. If you've got to stand alone, then you will. If you're married and your husband is not that way, you need to stand on God. Don't wait for your husband or your wife, you need to encourage yourself in the Lord. Having a family is hard. It's hard being married and raising children. It's hard being in a church where there are so many different personalities.

When people let you down, God wasn't caught by surprise! As a matter of fact, God was there, and possibly cheering them on. Do you believe that all things work together for good? Then act like it. Act like it when your best friend is not best friends with you anymore. Act like it when a good friend moves out of town or the other one betrayed you. Jesus was betrayed by Judas. He didn't say, "Father, I'm not going to die on the cross now! I am not going to die on the cross!" Where would we be if He had not died on the cross? We'd be lost.

Let me give you ten words for encouraging yourself in the Lord.

1. **Practical.** I'm a very practical person. Read 1 Kings 19:5–8. This is when Elijah the prophet was running away from Jezebel from a threat that she gave.

> Then as he lay and slept under a broom tree, suddenly an angel touched him, and said to him, "Arise and eat." Then he looked, and there by his head was a cake baked on coals, and a jar of water. So he ate and drank, and lay down again. And the angel of the Lord came back the second time, and touched him, and said, "Arise and eat, because the journey is too great for you." So he arose, and ate and drank; and he went in the strength of that food forty days and forty nights as far as Horeb, the mountain of God.

In 1 Kings 18, Elijah is God's man of faith and power. He challenges 350 prophets of Baal, beat them, and called down fire from the sky. But then he is physically depleted. He is physically, mentally, emotionally, and spiritually wiped out. His tank is not low, it's empty. It's a physiological fact that we human beings are not like animals. When there is danger or there's stress, our kidneys, our adrenal glands in our kidneys, secrete out a chemical called adrenaline. Adrenaline gives you strength and gives you power. I'm sure you've heard about some mothers who have even lifted up a car to get their kid out from being pinned underneath it. It's because of the adrenaline.

When I preach, hopefully I'm under the anointing, but the adrenaline goes out. Here's the problem: when adrenaline leaves your body, you become a "wet noodle." It takes two chemicals for your brain to function. They're called neurotransmitters. The two chemicals are dopamine and serotonin. Dopamine and serotonin are necessary for your brain to have its normal electrical current. As I am writing right now, it's going beep . . . beep . . . beep . . . beep. You need those neurochemicals, those neurotransmitters, in order to think and pick up things. When your adrenaline is used up, it's like you're on a downer. You don't want to be with people at that moment. Never make major decisions when you are in adrenaline withdrawal. Never make major decisions, because one of the consequences of adrenaline withdrawal is depression. When you're really tired, you've burned the candle at both ends. That's not the time to make a decision, because your decision would be: "No, leave me alone!" That adrenaline first needs to be restored.

We cannot function well with sleep deprivation. I must admit that I don't sleep very well. I have a tendency to stay up late and wake up early. Sometimes it's the Holy Spirit. I'll get up at two or three in the morning and when my eyes are just moist, I'm wide awake. I know it's the Lord waking me up, so I'll get up and pray. Most of the time it's not the Holy Spirit, though: I just can't sleep. Those times I just excuse myself and go somewhere, and that's not good. You can't survive on sleep deprivation for long. If you accumulate sleep deprivation, you will fall asleep driving behind the wheel. You can't focus and you don't have the attention you need to take care of what needs to be done. But the scriptures say that God gives us sleep; He gives us rest.

Pay attention to your bodily nutrition. When the widow baked the cake for Elijah, it was very nutritious food. So you must take care of yourself. If you're going to encourage yourself in the Lord you are never going to do it by drinking three Coca-colas a day, eating candy bars, stopping by the donut place, or by saying, "I'll have a coffee with four sugars." Do you understand what I am telling you? You are setting yourself up for the devil to really be able to hammer you. Drink lots of water: filtered water if possible. I drink lots of water every day. The majority of your body makeup is water.

You must also exercise. Walking is excellent exercise. You might ask, "Pastor, you're speaking on encouraging yourself in the Lord, what are you talking about all these things for?" Believe me; they're extremely relevant, because you need practical advice. They walked in those days, but we hardly ever walk today.

What's this got to do with hearing God? Everything. If you are malnourished, you don't have the capacity to hear God well. Take good vitamin supplements. I have got to be super-healthy, so I try to eat well by eating fish and balanced meals. I can't afford to walk into the pulpit in my church half-dilapidated. My church does not need a pastor like that. That's why I feel young.

2. **The Person of God**. God is not an "it," He's a person. I want you to know, go to the person of God. Go to God; He's a person. If you watch secular television or movies, you see that everybody uses God's name in vain. "Oh God" this, and "oh God" that. Sometimes I hear the

Lord saying, "They use My name," but almost like He's a swearing. He's a person.

You can hear God through His Word. You can encourage yourself through His Word. I've chosen some scriptures that are very encouraging. These are all meant for you to meditate on when you are in the valley of the dumps. Have you been there?

Part of Psalm 25:8–18 reads, "Good and upright is the Lord. Therefore he teaches sinners in the way. The humble He guides in justice." If I want to encourage myself in the Lord, I've got to be humble. Maybe God allowed me to be down in the dumps to keep me humble. "And the humble He teaches His way. All the paths of the Lord are mercy and truth, to such as keep His covenant and His testimonies. For your name's sake, O Lord, pardon my iniquity, for it is great. Who is the man that fears the Lord? Him shall He teach in the way He chooses. He himself shall dwell in prosperity. And his descendants shall inherit the earth."

Look at verse 14: "The secret of the Lord is with those who fear Him, and he will show them His covenant." Keep your fear of the Lord. By the way, do you fear His presence? Too often we fear His judgments. Two things will keep you in God: the love of God and the fear of God. There are days when I need his love, and there are days when I need his fear.

Then in verse 15: "My eyes are ever toward the Lord, for He shall pluck my feet out of the net." You must tell yourself: "God's going to pull me out of this net. I don't know when. Hurry up, Lord; take a hint. "Turn yourself to me, and have mercy on me for I am desolate and afflicted." Isn't that good? "The troubles of my heart have enlarged. Bring me out of my distresses. Look on my affliction and my pain, and forgive all my sins."

When you are troubled and nothing's going right, it's very easy to see your sins. When everything is going so good and we might get a little puffed up, it might be hard to talk to us at that time.

His word and His presence will greatly encourage you!

Another very encouraging scripture is Isaiah 26:3, "You will keep him in perfect peace, whose mind is stayed on You, because he trusts in you." Focus your mind on Jesus. Focus your attention on His Word. You will do what you think because your thoughts become words and your words become actions. Your actions become habits and your character, and your habits and character will determine your destiny.

It's extremely important what you think. My wife and I were watching the movie, "The Iron Lady," with Meryl Streep. It's the story of English Prime Minister Margaret Thatcher. It's an absolutely brilliant study. Margaret Thatcher actually was quoted as saying, "Everybody wants to know how you are feeling." But feelings are deceptive. How I'm feeling has nothing to do with what I'm doing.

That's why we have this prodigy of Facebook. Have you ever read some of the posts? "I feel miserable today." Honey, I don't want to read that. I don't want to read about your misery. Tell me what you're thinking, because what you're thinking is going to determine your talking, and your talking is going to determine your actions. Your actions will make habits and those habits will form a character and your character will form your destiny. We need to get out of the realm of only "How are you feeling today?"

Then we invented a word called *happy*. If whatever is happening is good, then we're happy. If whatever is happening is bad, then we're sad. Says who? We need to rise above feelings, because if you're going to encourage yourself in the Lord, you have to rise above your mood. Don't let your destiny be determined by moods, even by other people's moods. You need to let the Word of God determine your mood.

Keep your mind on God, and He will keep you in perfect peace. When you're down in the dumps, remind yourself that "the Lord will perfect that which concerns me" (Psalms 138:8).

Then add to that Philippians 1:6: "Being confident in this very thing, that He who has begun a good work in you will complete it until the day of Jesus Christ."

Wow! Based on those two scriptures, you can look in the mirror and say, "Do you know what? It's going to get better! It's going to get better because my God does not lie!" "God is not a man that He should lie" (Numbers 23:19).

If God says that He's going to perfect that which concerns me, He's going to do it! I'm going to cooperate with Him as long as He does it. Even if I don't see Him doing it, I'm going to cooperate with God.

3. **The Purpose of God.** Whenever you're going through something where you need to encourage yourself in the Lord, you've got to learn to ask the right questions. A lot of people say, "God, why me?" The next questions are: "How long?" and "What did I do to deserve this?" Those are the wrong questions to ask. The right question to ask is: What can I learn from this? Here's another question: Which thoughts am I going to share with God?

Am I going to say, "Where are You?" Or am I going to say, "This is exciting, God. Surprise me, because we're doing this together." "Okay

God, what is the purpose of my current affliction?" If Romans 8:28 is true, if all things work together for good, then what can I learn from this situation? I may not see any good in it. I may not see any purpose, but I'm going to keep looking until I find the good.

Good number 1: It sure has humbled me.

Good number 2: I haven't been praying much lately, but I am now.

Good number 3: I was taking You for granted, Lord, but now You've got my attention.

Just maybe there is a purpose of God for this affliction. Ask Him. Then please journal during that time. By the way, David had no time to journal during that time they had the rocks in their hands, so David was in a regular habit of worshipping. That's what saved him.

Ask: "God, if You're allowing this, how is this affecting my ministry?" You might say, "Well, I don't have a ministry!" Sure you do. Everybody has a ministry. God has given gifts to you. Find out what they are. Second Timothy 1:9 reads, "Who has saved us and called us with a Holy calling, not according to our works, but according to His own purpose and grace which was given to us in Christ before time began."

Did you know that before the world began you had a Holy calling?

Then you have to ask yourself this, in your discouragement, "What is the purpose of Satan?" What do you think the devil is trying to do? You have to remember that the devil is not everywhere; the devil is not omnipresent. Don't give him credit where credit is not due. Only God is everywhere. Now there are demons all over the place. If you are negative by nature, the devil doesn't even have to attack you, you do that to yourself. You may be one of those people, who, whenever anything goes wrong, immediately say, "We're all dead; it's all over now!" I tell some people I need to lay hands on them. They respond: "Oh, do you think I have a spirit?" I say, "No, I think I need to slap you! Just stop it!"

John 10:10: "The thief does not come except to steal, kill and destroy." Jesus said, "I have come that they may have life and they may have it more abundantly." The Greek word for life there is *zoe*, like the name Zoe: it means life on the highest level that you are capable of.

There are four things that Satan wants to do, and you must remember this when you are being discouraged. He wants to destroy you. I mean both physically and spiritually. He will take anything you give him. Don't let Satan destroy you. If he can't destroy you, he will distract you. That's why you're feeling so discouraged. If he can't distract you, he'll cause you distress. Some people will say that the devil will just freak them out to cause them to panic. The devil wants you in the realm of, "What are we going to do now?" He wants to see you depressed. He would love to see you to try and take your life.

Then there are people who supposedly figure out that, if they find another church, maybe they'll be happier. But you know what? You'll find the same people in that church, too. The important thing is not what happens *to* me, it's what happens *in* me. We must learn that! You should only leave if that's where the Lord is leading. Encourage yourself! Ask yourself, what is the purpose in this affliction? There's got to be a lesson here. All things do work together for good.

So you begin to identify the good. What lessons am I learning? Patience; for one. Second, how this is affecting my ministry. Maybe it will make me more sensitive to people. Maybe my people skills are lacking, and I need to improve them.

How about this one? "But God, it wasn't my fault!" Now He's showing me how He feels, because when we do things to Him, it wasn't His fault, either.

4. **Pardon.** Pardon means forgiveness. Ephesians 1:7 reads, "In Him we have redemption through His blood, the forgiveness of sins, according to the riches of His grace."

There are four things I want to show you, because hard times are good times to look inside. You are never more humble than when you're suffering. "God, I'm going to stay humble so I don't have to go through the hard times. I want to stay humble; I don't want another hard time, all right? I've had enough hard times."

Here is what you must remember: Every time you repent, God forgives you. You question: "David Garcia, do you mean every time?" I said: EVERY TIME.

First John 1:9 says, "If we confess our sins, He is faithful and just to forgive us our sins and to cleanse us from all unrighteousness." You might say, "Well, I'm not a sinner." 1 John 1:8 says, if you say you have no sin, you're a liar. Everybody on earth sins. But you must remember that God forgives you every time. But here's the second part: therefore you have to forgive yourself. Do you have a natural tendency—when you've blown it and this is not the first time, maybe it's the tenth time—you say "How could I have been so stupid? How could I have done that? I knew better. I was looking to not do it, but I did it anyway!" Welcome to the Christian club; "oh wretched man that I am," as it says in Romans 7. You have to forgive yourself.

Third, I must get over my mistakes. Did you ever lay something down and you didn't know where you put it? You ask your husband or your wife, "Did you take my cell phone? I'm telling you I put it right here; which one of you took my cell phone?" How about your keys?; and then you find them in your pocket. Then you have to go around to all those in your family, including the dog, to tell them you are sorry. Did you ever do that? Of course you have.

Therefore, we must get over the mistakes of others. Granted, we all blow it at times; we are human. Do Christians drive badly sometimes? Yes. The problem is they may drive badly and cut you off and fight you for the parking spot at Wal-Mart during the holiday season. Many people, including Christians, are going to mess up. Encourage yourself in the Lord by saying, "You know, they are only human and, more important, I'm only human." We forgive ourselves and them, and we keep on going.

5. **Prayers.** Psalm 10:1 reads: "Why do you stand so far off, O Lord? Why do you hide in times of trouble?"

Have you ever felt that way? I know I have felt that way many times. Those are the times when you've got to pray. Read all of Psalms 77, and be encouraged in the Lord. When you are encouraging yourself in the Lord is the perfect time to talk to God. The Bible says, in 1 Thessalonians 5:17, to "pray without ceasing." That says it all. Those three words are extremely important and are very direct. It's not open to any theological interpretation. It's time for you to pray.

6. **Praise**. Praise is the opposite of what you feel when you're down. Are you human? Then when you feel down, you want to complain. You don't want to celebrate God. But you have to force yourself. Praise Him for what He has done in the past. That's why it's good to keep a journal. Do you remember when you were

healed? "Yeah, but I'm sick right now. I've got the flu bug." But do you remember when you were healed? Do you remember when you were saved? Do you remember when He gave you that check from the IRS that you weren't expecting? He did it before. He'll do it again. So praise Him for what He's doing now.

Resist self-pity! Get up! Joshua, get up; stop feeling sorry for yourself. Self-pity really multiplies when you tell yourself that "nobody else is going through this," and you think that you are the only one! When we feel sorry for ourselves, we exaggerate everything. Nobody seems to understand us. "My wife just doesn't understand me!" "My husband just doesn't understand me!" She probably understands you a whole lot more than you are giving her credit for—that's why she's staying away from you!

7. **Possibility**. "Come on, let's get out of this dump." You need to focus on possibility. If you focus on impossibility, if you keep focusing on what's going wrong, you will be greatly discouraged. Focus on what's going right: I'm saved, I'm sanctified, I'm baptized in the Holy Spirit! I've got the power of life and death in my mouth!

Romans 4:17–21 says: "God who gives life to the dead and call those things which do not exist as though they did; [Abraham], contrary to hope, in hope believed, so that he became the father of many nations, according to what was spoken, 'So shall your descendants be. And not being weak in faith, he did not consider his own body, already dead (since he was about a hundred years old), and the deadness of Sarah's womb. He did not waiver at the promise of God through unbelief, but was strengthened in faith, giving glory to God, and being fully convinced that what He had promised He was also able to perform."

Tell yourself that when you're going through hard times. Say "I'm not considering my own situation!" Hallelujah! That's what I have got to think about! I must think about Hebrews 11:6: "But without faith it is impossible to please God, for he who comes to God must believe that He is and that He is a rewarder of those who diligently seek Him."

You must think about 1 John 5:4: "Whatever is born of God overcomes the world." Are you saved? Then overcome the world! This is a victory, to overcome the world.

Joshua 1:8 reads: "This Book of the Law shall not depart from your mouth, but you shall meditate in it day and night, that you may observe to do according to all that is written in it. For then YOU will make your way prosperous, and then YOU will have good success.[emphasis mine].

Did you understand that scripture? When I'm down in the dumps, the Bible doesn't belong in my heart, it belongs in my mouth. There are three crucial words there: mind, meditation, and mouth.

Remember, my thoughts will become an action and my action becomes a habit. Your meditation is your thoughts. You've got to meditate on God's Word. Don't meditate on the situation: you'll go crazy doing that. Don't meditate on, "I'm three months behind in the mortgage. God, my house!" Whose house? It's His; it's His house. You've got to absolutely focus on those things.

8. **Patience**. I can't speak about you, but when I'm desperate and discouraged I want help last week, not yesterday; I want it now! You want it now. Hurting people want things now! Jesus says in Luke 21:19, "By your patience possess your souls." What's your soul? Your

mind, emotions, and your will. In patience, put your thoughts under the obedience of Jesus. Don't let some wild thoughts come in, such as "It's all over now!"

Put your emotions under the obedience of God's Word. Put your decisions under the will of God. Use patience, and think about waiting this out. God is in control because you belong to God. Think about these two things:

Number 1: I can out-wait the devil. The devil's the one who's running out of time. The devil is the one who realizes that at any moment Jesus is coming. So we can out-wait the devil. He doesn't have a lot of time; he's the one who's in a hurry. Why should you be in a hurry?

Number 2. Realize that this, too, will pass. This is going to pass. I like that scripture, "and it came to pass." Do you remember the last tight spot you were in? Do you remember how bad it was? Do you remember how God works if you don't do something? You are still here. We have to learn this important lesson that our lives are in God's hands!

What's the worst thing that can happen? You're dead; and where will you be when you're dead? You'll be in Heaven. That's promotion. Christians are the only people that they all want to go to Heaven, but no one wants to die. What is the worst thing that can happen? In Hebrews 2:14–16 it says, "He delivered us from the bondage of the fear of death." Once you realize that you are not scared of dying, what else can the devil do to you? You're going to Heaven.

People ask me, "When you go overseas, are you not scared that some terrorist is going to kill you?" No, because if they do, I'm going to Heaven. So don't worry about it.

9. **Prophecy.** Ask God to bless your church and to move in the prophetic. Do you remember the prophecies given to you personally? Paul told Timothy in 1 Timothy 4:14, "Do not neglect the gift that is in you which was given to you by prophecy with the laying on of hands of the eldership." I remember when I first came to my church over one-quarter century ago. Within two or three weeks after my arrival, a prophet came and prophesied to me in front of the whole church. He told me about my whole ministry, and prophesied to the church. There are many times in my twenty-five years that I've leaned on that prophecy. God called me, not man.

Another prophecy told to me—I think in 1974—that from this little church the light of the gospel would go to the four corners of the earth. There were only between 70 and 100 people in my church at the time. I still remember that prophecy. I still depend on that prophecy. That prophecy is not "going" to happen, it IS happening!

Recall the prophecies of the last days. What are we worried about? Discouraging people tell us that the country is going broke and this and that. But my God is still on the throne. God is still alive. There are going to be tsunamis, earthquakes, etc.; Jesus said they were going to happen. Get excited, because it's just a sign that the Lord is coming! I shouldn't get down, I should get up!

10. **Power.** You need the practical word of the power of God. God's got power over what we don't. 1 John 4:4 declares, "Greater is He that is in you then he that is in the world!" I've got power! I can speak to this storm.

You know what? I can speak to depression, "Leave me in Jesus name!"

2 Corinthians 10:3–5 says that I can bring every thought that's against the word of God under the obedience of Jesus! So depression, in Jesus name, bow down to the will of God right now! Emotions, terror, and fear, I command you to be under the blood of Jesus. Remember, Jesus said that John the Baptist was a great prophet, but he that is in the kingdom is greater than John the Baptist. God said about John, no other mother ever gave birth to a prophet greater than John the Baptist, and yet we are greater than John the Baptist because we can do something that John couldn't. We can stop a storm. We can command a demon to leave.

AFTERWORD

YOU'VE GOT POWER IN YOU that no Old Testament prophet had. Don't let the newspaper headlines or nightly news scare you or depress you.

I like what Marilyn Hickey says: "I don't watch the news, I change the news!"[19]

Be encouraged today!

Be a powerful last-day Christian!

Be an overcomer!

Will you really look at people and see them and encourage them, just like Christ admonished you to do: "Therefore encourage one another and build each other up, just as in fact you are doing." (1 Thessalonians 5:11 NIV)

Stand up and be a powerful last-day Christian today!

Please pray this final prayer with me:

FATHER, IN JESUS NAME, HOW wonderful is the Lord! Thank you for these words to encourage ourselves in the Lord. I pray against the power of depression right now in the name of Jesus. I command every form of discouragement to be loosed from my dear reader right now, in Jesus name! I

---

[19] Marilyn Hickey, "Today with Marilyn and Sarah" television program, 2010, Daystar Television Network.

command every countenance to be lifted up right now. God, my demeanor doesn't have to be influenced by what people do or don't do, because I've got God inside of me!

MY SITUATION IS GOING TO turn around. It cannot stay the same!

LORD GOD, I GIVE YOU my thoughts. Let my thoughts sow Biblical words, let my words result in Biblical actions, let my actions result in Biblical habits, and my habits result in a Biblical character, and let my character determine my destiny: where I'll walk on streets of gold and have my own mansion and have my own assignment. I thank you God!

HELP ME TO BE A powerful last-day Christian!

TO BECOME A CHRISTIAN:

If you have not made your simple, yet eternal, decision to become a Christian, you can make it right now! It is so profound, so eternal, yet in many cases, so simple. Pray with me right now:

LORD JESUS, I BELIEVE YOU died for my sins and I ask Your forgiveness. I receive You now as my personal Savior and invite You to manage my life from this day forward. Amen.

God wants to give you a new life of peace and victory. God wants to give you the peace that passes all human understanding. By faith, receive what God has already done for YOU!

If this book has been a blessing to you, please let me know.

Pastor David Garcia
20366 Cortez Road
Brooksville, FL 34601
pastorgarcia@graceworldag.org

ABOUT THE AUTHOR

David Garcia is the Lead Pastor of one of central Florida's most exciting churches, Grace World Outreach Church, located in Brooksville, Florida for over one-quarter century.

For 35 years, Pastor Garcia has been blessed with unique insight into God's word and an exceptional preach-teach style of presenting it. He possesses a prophetic gifting that speaks directly to the heart of the listener. His anointing flows in evangelism with signs and wonders confirming the Word.

Pastor Garcia is a versatile and popular seminar, crusade, and conference speaker who offers a wealth of Biblical and practical ideas. He is also a gifted author with a unique style of relevant presentation.

David is also the leader of The Hands of God Ministry, which facilitates his international travel ministry and helps him to serve as an advisor and spiritual father to ministries in the Philippines, Mexico, Tanzania, and to pastors throughout the United States.

He brings his New York City "street smarts" raising, coupled with his miraculous salvation and the experience gained following God's call to the mission field in Zimbabwe, Africa, to the compassionate pastoral style that he is so well-known for. David and his wife, Nellie, have been married for 44 years and have two happily married children, both serving God in full-time ministry, and four wonderful grandchildren.

For more information about
David Garcia
&

Portrait of a Powerful Last-Day Christian:
Prophetic Insights for Successful End-Time Living
please visit:

gwocag.org
pastorgarcia@graceworldag.org

For more information about
AMBASSADOR INTERNATIONAL
please visit:

www.ambassador-international.com
@AmbassadorIntl
www.facebook.com/AmbassadorIntl